CAMP DAVID ACCORDS

Clete Hinton

EAGLE EDITIONS
2008

EAGLE EDITIONS
AN IMPRINT OF HERITAGE BOOKS, INC.

Books, CDs, and more—Worldwide

For our listing of thousands of titles see our website at
www.HeritageBooks.com

Published 2008 by
HERITAGE BOOKS, INC.
Publishing Division
100 Railroad Ave. #104
Westminster, Maryland 21157

Copyright © 1980 Clete A. Hinton

Other books by the author:
Arc of Crisis 1979
Return of the Sinai 1979
CD: Arc of Crisis 1979
CD: Return of the Sinai 1979

All rights reserved. No part of this book may be reproduced or transmitted in any form or by any means, electronic or mechanical, including photocopying, recording or by any information storage and retrieval system without written permission from the author, except for the inclusion of brief quotations in a review.

International Standard Book Numbers
Paperbound: 978-0-7884-2515-8
Clothbound: 978-0-7884-7483-5

DEDICATION

To all people who believe that peace is possible in our time and in this world.

CONTENTS

Foreword: Biographical Sketches

1. Origin and History of the Jewish State 1
2. Preview of the Middle East before the Camp David Accords 5
3. A Framework for Peace in the Middle East 11
4. Letters Leading to the Camp David Accords 23
5. Events following the Camp David Accords 31
6. History of the Path to Peace 97
7. The Egyptian-Israeli Peace Treaty 101
8. Conclusion 105

Bibliography 107

FOREWORD: Biographical Sketches

Menachem Begin (1913-) Prime Minister of Israel.

Menachem Begin, who was born in Poland, is one of the few survivors of the generation of elder statesmen who helped bring the Jewish State into existence. Begin took office as the sixth Prime Minister on June 21, 1977. He commanded an underground army in the revolt against the British in the pre-independence period, and gained a worldwide reputation as a terrorist. He demonstrates a greater flexibility now than in the past, and he has gained eminence as "a leader of unquestioned domestic strength."

In 1948, shortly after the State of Israel was proclaimed, Begin formed a political party called the "Herut" (The Freedom Movement). This party was a coalition which eventually became part of the Knesset (ruling body of Israel). The main goal of Prime Minister Menachem Begin is "Peace with all nations."

His wife is the former Aliza Arnold, whom he married in Poland in 1939. They have one son, two daughters, and several grandchildren. Begin is a devoted family man. He also is a man of "principle and honor."

Cyrus R. Vance (1917-   )

Cyrus R. Vance is the United States Secretary of State, nominated on December 3, 1976. Vance is a quiet, self-effacing team player, who believes that the Secretary of State should delegate key responsibility. Vance was born in Clarksville, West Virginia. He is a former Wall Street lawyer, and counsellor for Senate committees, who served with distinction as General Counsel for the Defense Department.

Vance was President Johnson's personal envoy during crisis situations, (Deputy Secretary of Defense) at home and abroad. In 1968-69 he was Deputy Chief Delegate to the Paris Peace talks on Vietnam. He was a member of the peacemaking team sent to Panama after the Canal Zone police forcibly quelled demonstrations by Panamanian students in 1964.

As an undergraduate, he majored in economics at Yale University. Vance is a graduate of Kent State Law School. He was a member of Kent State's football, ice hockey, and rowing teams.

His wife is the former Grace Sloane, whom he married on February 15, 1947. They have four children. Vance is an impeccable dresser. He is modest, strong yet sympathetic, and he works for "solid achievement."

President James Carter (1924-   )

President James Carter is the 39th President of the United States. He took office on January 20, 1977. Carter is very liberal on human rights, civil rights, and environmental quality, but he is conservative on management of government. Domestically, he has proceeded with a combination of fiscal caution and progressive concern, trying to stimulate the economy, while he attempts to reduce unemployment.

The President was born in Plains, Georgia, on October 1, 1924. He entered Anapolis Naval Academy in 1943. He applied for the nuclear submarine program in 1951, under Admiral Rickover, and he was accepted.

In his first bid for elected office, Carter ran for the Georgia Senate, but was narrowly defeated. He became "a born again Christian" in 1966. He stated: "I had a profound religious experience that changed my life pragmatically, and I recognized that I lacked something very precious — a complete commitment to Christ, and the presence of the Holy Spirit."

On January 21, 1971, Carter became Governor of Georgia. As Governor, he opened the Georgia Senate and legislature to women and minorities, especially blacks. He established environmental controls, introduced a merit system for cabinet and judicial appointments, improved prison rehabilitation programs, established day-care centers for the mentally retarded, and established several drug abuse clinics.

The President keeps in shape by playing tennis and softball. He dresses in comfortable clothes during his times of leisure activities.

President Carter married the former Rosalyn Smith of Plains, Georgia, on July 7, 1946. They have four children. Carter teaches a Bible class at the First Baptist church in Washington, D.C.

Anwar El Sadat (1918-   )

Anwar El Sadat is President of the United Arab Republic. After the fatal heart attack of Gamal Abdel Nassar on September 28, 1970, who was Egypt's leader for almost two decades, and one of the most powerful Arab leaders, Anwar Sadat, with an impressive show of political stability, became the President of the Arab Republic. He was sworn into office on October 17, 1970, for a six-year term. For several years prior to his election, he served as editor for Egypt's semi-official newspaper, *Al Gomhuriya*. Sadat also held posts in the government, and was vice-president when Nassar died.

He was born in Talah Monufiya, a village in the Nile Delta, of poor but devout Moslem parents. As a youth, Sadat longed to become an army officer. He met Gamal Nassar at Abbassia Military Academy in 1936, and the two became close friends.

Sadat was a member of the Presidential Council of Nassar from 1962-4. He was Secretary General of the

Islamic Congress, and in 1969, President Nassar named Anwar Sadat to vice-president of the Arab Republic. In 1971 Sadat dedicated the Aswan Dam, a project that took more than ten years to build, to Gamal Nassar.

Anwar is married and has three daughters and a son by his present wife, Jihan. He also has three daughters by a previous marriage. The President of Egypt is charming and genial in manner. He is an avid reader, who enjoys reading books on Islamic culture, as well as novels by Lloyd Douglas and Zane Grey. Sadat has written an unpublished political novel entitled, "The Prince of the Island."

Other members of the peace making process who were involved in the negotiations are:
In Egypt: Vice-President Hosny Mubarak, and Prime Minister Mustafa Khalil.
In Israel: Foreign Minister, Moshe Dayan, and Defense Minister Ezer Weizman.
In United States: Under Secretary of State, Alfred Atherton.

Chapter 1

ORIGIN AND HISTORY OF THE JEWISH STATE

Although Israel is one of the youngest states in the world, it is still among the oldest. Other peoples have recovered their independence after centuries of subjugation, but they existed as a compact entity, living on their own soil, speaking their own language, and enjoying a greater or lesser degree of autonomy. The Jews, on the other hand, had to recover not only their sense of nationhood, but also their language. They were transplanted physically to a land from which they had been estranged for more than two thousand years. The history of the Jewish state begins in Europe.

After the destruction of Judea in the first century A.D., Jews fled in all directions: some went eastward toward the ancient Jewish communities of Babylon; others moved westward to Egypt, and from there traveled across the Mediterranean to Spain, Italy, and France.

Wherever they settled, they usually found they were under the rule of Rome. They preserved their own way of life, their rituals, their exclusiveness, and their unique identity.

Throughout the centuries from the fall of Jerusalem until our own times, the Jew has moved from one place to another. Tolerance brought an influx; oppression forced an exodus.

The first pogrom (organized attack) was perpetrated in France and the Rhineland in 1096 A.D. by Crusaders enroute to the Holy Land. The Jews were gradually reduced to pariahs (social outcasts).

The Jews were driven out of France and Spain into Germany, Poland and the Ukraine, and Austria. Only in Poland were the Jewish people treated with respect and dignity. These conditions existed until the turn of the seventeenth century. The incursions of the Cossacks from the Ukrainian territories of the Polish Empire devastated the Jewish community. A number of Jewish refugees, approximately five million, were placed under Russian rule.

Throughout his varying change of fortune, the Jew maintained an unswerving loyalty to his faith, and among the basic elements of that faith is a belief in the return to Zion (the Israelites whose religious life is centered on Mount Zion).

Prayers for the rebuilding of Jerusalem were said, and still are said three times a day. They are contained in the grace after meals, and expressions of longing for Zion appear and reappear in the Sabbath and festive liturgy. The "Day of Atonement," the most sacred day in the Jewish year, concludes with the hope of, "The next year in Jerusalem."

This Zionism is Messianic. The restoration of the Jews in Judea will come about through divine intervention. The Jews intone, "I shall await his coming daily," in their prayers.

A Jewish editor by the name of Herzl published in his *Judenstaat (Jewish State)* in 1896, his advocacy of a "Society of Jews," a means to organize the mass movement of Jews toward their homeland, and a "Jewish company" to finance this movement.

The idea of a Jewish State continued to grow and stimulated the interest of an English Foreign Secretary, Lord Balfour, and he wrote to Lord Rothchild in 1917. His letter was encouraging to the Zionist movement. He wrote: "His Majesty's government views with favor the establishment in Palestine of a national home for the Jewish people, and will use their best endeavors to facilitate the achievement of this object, it being clearly understood that nothing shall be done which may prejudice the civil and religious rights of existing non-Jewish communities in Palestine, or the rights and political status enjoyed by Jews in any other country. Zionism had won its charter, but it was only the beginning."

Settlements were established in Palestine and were called "Kibbutzim," embodying the principle, "from each according to his ability, to each according to his needs." No wages are paid, and all work, property, and amenities are shared. They were principally agricultural enterprises, but many Kibbutzim have profitable factories, workshops, and guest houses.

The immigration of the Jewish people began in earnest. They came from all over the world to Palestine, and they still continue to arrive in Jerusalem and the surrounding area of Mount Zion.

In May 1948, under the chairmanship of David Ben Gurion, the State of Israel was proclaimed. The Charter stated:

"The State will be open to all immigrants, will promote the development of the country for all its inhabitants, will be based on the precepts of liberty, justice and peace taught by the Hebrew prophets, will uphold full social and political equality for all its citizens without distinction of race, creed or sex, and will guarantee full freedom of education and culture."

The military force of Israel called the "Hagana" grew in size and strength, with conscription of both men and women. The length of National Service varied, depending on the circumstances. Men remain on the reserve list until they are 49, and women until they are 34. The men must report annually for a month's training.

The ruling body of the State of Israel is called a Knesset, an assembly of 120 members elected by a simple majority for a period of five years. A member of the Knesset signs international treaties, receives ambassadors and visiting heads of state, and may exercise the prerogative of pardon. During a political crisis he will intervene to obtain a settlement.

The first Prime Minister of Israel was David Ben Gurion, born in Plonsk, Poland, in 1886, who settled in Palestine 20 years later. He was one of the pioneers of the Second Aliya (a collective settlement), and he worked as a laborer in the vineyards of Rishon Le Zion. In 1910, he became the editor of a weekly labor paper, a lawyer at the Ottoman School of Law, and he later joined the American battalion of the Jewish Legion as a soldier. He was instrumental in creating the General Federation of Labor, the *Histadrut* ("state within a state"), and he became its General Secretary. He formulated the Biltmore Program, endorsed by the Zionist General Council, giving the Jewish people a powerful militant organization.

THE SIX DAY WAR — 1967

In a fight for survival of the Jewish State of Israel, the army of the Jewish people attacked the Arab air bases in Egypt, Syria, Jordan, and Iraq on the morning of June 5, 1967, and destroyed over 400 airplanes on the ground. There were fierce tank battles in Sinai and the Gaza strip. By the end of the first day Israel had extended her army to the Gaza Strip. The city of Gaza fell on the second day, and the Israelis marched 40 miles inside Sinai. On the third day they took Sharm El Sheik near the Sinai Peninsula, overlooking the Straits of Tiran. The city of Jerusalem (old city) was reunited with New Jerusalem, and after nearly 2,000 years the Jews were once again in full control of the City of David. On the eleventh of June the fighting with the Arabians was over. The victory for the Israelis was swift, sure, and complete.

Chapter 2

PREVIEW OF THE MIDDLE EAST BEFORE THE CAMP DAVID ACCORDS

The Middle East:
In an article written by Harold H. Saunders, Assistant Secretary for Near Eastern and South Asian Affairs, "The Middle East," Mr. Saunders tells us what is at stake today in the Middle East, and how our perceptions of this area have evolved over the last three decades.

After the Second World War, our thoughts ran along two lines. First, we considered the strategic front. We thought in terms of physical geography, characterizing the Middle East as "the strategic crossroads" or as a "land bridge," joining Europe and Asia and Africa. This perception grew out of prewar European political concepts and the experience of a generation that fought in the Middle East and North Africa and across the Mediterranean during the war. The later Soviet thrusts in Iran, Turkey, and Greece to expand their postwar influence reinforced this view.

Then in 1948 we committed ourselves to the existence and to the survival of Israel as a Jewish State, and as a home for victims of the Holocaust and others who wished to come, and as an active, alive, and independent democracy.

By the early 1960s, the advent of intercontinental missiles with nuclear warheads caused us to shift from seeing national interest primarily in terms of the Middle East's geographic position to a perception of the Middle East in global strategy. We wanted to enhance our influence in the area partly because the Mediterranean remained an important lifeline to our NATO allies and our allies to the East, but also because of the importance of oil to Western Europe. Direct U.S. interests, apart from the availability of oil to our allies at reasonable prices, largely centered in oil-related activities.

The United States also continued its firm commitment to Israel's strength and well-being and, at the same time, expressed humanitarian concern for peace in the Middle East which would permit all the people of the area, including the displaced Palestinians, to build better lives.

Preventing Conflict:
We have long recognized that it is imperative that the United States seek to prevent conflict in the Middle East from again becoming a flashpoint, and that helping strengthen the independence of Middle Eastern countries will contribute to stability in the region and make war less likely.

Since the mid-1960s the Arab-Israeli wars of 1967 and 1973 have demonstrated to us in the heat of crisis that the Middle East is an area where U.S. and Soviet forces could confront each other in the context of a local war. Now, with estimates of the Soviet Union's own changing energy needs, a new dimension has been added to the traditional Soviet interest in a strong position in that area.

Israel's Security:
Our irrevocable commitment to the security, strength, and well-being of Israel has been reaffirmed by every American administration since the modern State of Israel was born 30 years ago. It is a permanent feature of American foreign policy.

Today, however, Israel and United States must face together new and more difficult circumstances. Israel's security can be guaranteed over the long term by a policy of continued military strength coupled with a peaceful relationship with its neighbors. Close American cooperation with key Arab states is essential to achieving and guaranteeing peace.

The opportunity for peace has increased dramatically since President Sadat's historic trip to Jerusalem, and Israel's warm reception. The President of Egypt broke out of the 30 year cycle of war and truce to create a new psychological climate in which there can be progress toward peace between Israel and all its neighbors.

This area is no longer seen as simply a refugee problem; it is a problem of fulfilling the legitimate rights of the Palestinian people in ways that enable them to participate in the determination of their own future and to live in peace and security with Israel.

PREVIEW OF THE CAMP DAVID AGREEMENT

The framework for peace produced at Camp David by President Anwar Sadat of Egypt, Prime Minister Begin of Israel, and President Anwar Sadat of Egypt, Prime Minister Begin of Israel, and President Carter of the United States provides an unprecedented opportunity for the people of the Middle East to turn away from the long and tragic course of conflict, tension, and terror that has afflicted the Israelis and Arabs, as well as the world at large. President Carter explains:

"There are still great difficulties that remain and many hard issues to be settled. The questions that have brought warfare and bitterness to the Middle East for the last 30 years will not be dissolved overnight. We should all recognize the substantial achievements that have been made."

The effort at Camp David of the President was conducted in a spirit of humility, perseverance, and a deep sense of responsibility to the American people, the nations and peoples of the Middle East, and the cause of peace, justice, and progress.

No international agreement can succeed unless it provides a balance of benefits. Each party must be able to perceive that its particular interests are addressed seriously and with a sense of reciprocal advantage and responsibility.

Israel:
Support for a secure, free, and democratic Israel in the Middle East has been and will always be a permanent feature of American foreign policy. Indeed, it is a moral commitment by our country and a strategic concern. The ties of friendship that bind our two nations will be strengthened by the Camp David agreements.

The Camp David agreements go further toward meeting the fundamental concerns of Israel than any other international action since the founding of the modern State of Israel.

For Israel, these agreements speak to the centuries-old aspiration of the Jewish people to live in peace in a state of their own in the land of their forefathers, within secure and recognized borders, and to take their rightful place in the international community of nations.

The framework agreements also contain another indispensable element: arrangements to guarantee the security of the parties.
In the Sinai:
   A wide demilitarized zone.
   A limited armament zone east of the Suez canal.
   U.N. forces to assure freedom of passage through the Tiran Strait and as a buffer between Sinai and Gaza.
   U.N. forces in a zone along the Egyptian-Israeli border and the Gulf of Aqaba.
   Relocation of Israeli airfields east of the border, in the Negev desert.
   A small limited armament zone on the Israeli side of the border.

In the West Bank and Gaza:
Israeli security forces will remain in specified security

locations to provide for Israel's security.
There will be arrangements for insuring internal security.
There will be a 5 year interim period before the final status of the area is decided.
Israel has a voice, together with Egypt, Jordan, and the Palestinians, in the determination of the final results.

Chapter 3

A FRAMEWORK FOR PEACE IN THE MIDDLE EAST

Muhammad Anwar El Sadat, President of the Arab republic of Egypt, and Menachem Begin, Prime Minister of Israel, met with Jimmy Carter, President of the United States of America, at Camp David from September 5 to September 17, 1978. They have agreed to the following framework for peace in the Middle East, and they have invited other parties to the Arab-Israeli conflict to adhere to it:

Preamble
The search for peace in the Middle East must be guided by the following:
The agreed basis for a peaceful settlement of the conflict between Israel and its neighbors is the United Nations Security Council Resolution #242, and all its parts.
After four wars during thirty years, despite intensive human effort, the Middle East, which is the cradle of civilization and the birthplace of three great religions, does not yet enjoy the blessings of peace. The people of the Middle East yearn for peace so that the vast human and natural resources of the region can be turned to the pursuits of peace and so that this area can become a

model for co-existence and cooperation among nations.
The historic initiative of President Sadat in visiting Jerusalem, and the reception accorded to him by the parliament, government and people of Israel, and the reciprocal visit of Prime Minister Begin to Ismailia, the peace proposal made by both leaders, as well as the warm reception of these missions by the peoples of both countries, have created an unprecedented opportunity for peace which must not be lost, if this generation and future generations are to be spared the tragedies of war.
The provisions of the charter of the United Nations and other accepted norms of International Law and Legitimacy now provide accepted standards for the conduct of relations among all states.
To achieve a relationship of peace, in the spirit of Article #2 of the United Nations charter, future negotiations between Israel and any neighbor prepared to negotiate peace and security with it, are necessary for the purpose of carrying out all the provisions and principles of Resolutions #242 and #338.
Peace requires respect for the sovereignty, territorial integrity and political independence of every state in the area and their right to live in peace within secure and recognized boundaries free from threats or acts of force. Progress toward that goal can accelerate movement toward a new era of reconciliation in the Middle East marked by cooperation in promoting economic development, and maintaining stability, and assuring security.
Security is enhanced by a relationship of peace and by cooperation between nations which enjoy normal relations. In addition, under the terms of peace treaties, the parties can, on the basis of reciprocity, agree to special security arrangements such as demilitarized zones, limited armaments areas, early warning stations, the presence of international forces, liasons, agreed measures for monitoring, and other arrangements that they agree are useful.

Framework:
Taking these factors into account, the parties are

determined to reach a just, comprehensive, and durable settlement of the Middle East conflict through the conclusion of peace treaties based on Security Council Resolutions #242 and #338 in all their parts. Their purpose is to achieve peace and good neighborly relations. They recognize that, for peace to endure, it must involve all those who have been most affected by the conflict. They therefore agree that this framework as appropriate is intended by them to constitute a basis for peace between Israel and each of its other neighbors prepared to negotiate peace with Israel on this basis. With that objective in mind, they have agreed to proceed as follows:

A. West Bank and Gaza

1. Egypt, Israel, Jordan, and the representatives of the Palestinian people should participate in negotiations on the resolution of the Palestinian problem in all its aspects. To achieve that objective, negotiations relating to the West Bank and Gaza should proceed in three stages:

    a. Egypt and Israel agree that, in order to insure a peaceful and orderly transfer of authority, and taking into account the security concerns of all the parties, there should be transitional arrangements for the West Bank and Gaza for a period not exceeding five years. In order to provide full autonomy to the inhabitants, under these arrangements the Israeli military government and its civilian administration will be withdrawn as soon as a self-governing authority has been freely elected by the inhabitants of these areas to replace the existing military government. To negotiate the details of a transitional arrangement, the government of Jordan will be invited to join the negotiations on the basis of this framework. These new arrangements should give due consideration both to the principle of self-government by the inhabitants of these territories and to the legitimate security concerns of the parties involved.

    b. Egypt, Israel, and Jordan will agree on the modalities for establishing the elected self-governing authority in the West Bank and Gaza. The delegations of Egypt and Jordan may include Palestinians as mutually agreed. The parties will negotiate an agreement which will define the powers and responsibilities of the self-governing authority to be exercised in the West Bank and Gaza. A withdrawal of Israeli armed forces will take place and there will be a redeployment of the remaining Israeli forces into a specified security location. The agreement will also include arrangements for assuring internal and external security and public order. A strong local police force will be established, which may include Jordanian citizens. In addition Israeli and Jordanian forces will participate in joint patrols and in the manning of control posts to assure the security of the borders.

c. When the self-governing authority (administrative council) in the West Bank and Gaza is established and inaugurated, the transitional period of five years will begin. As soon as possible, but not later than the third year after the beginning of the transitional period, negotiations will take place to determine the final status of the West Bank and Gaza and its relationship with its neighbors, and to conclude a peace treaty between Israel and Jordan by the end of the transitional period. These negotiations will be conducted among Egypt, Israel, Jordan and the elected representatives of the inhabitants of the West Bank and Gaza. Two separate but related committees will be convened: one committee, consisting of the representatives of the four parties which will negotiate and agree on the final status of the West Bank and Gaza and its relationship with its neighbors; and the second committee, consisting of representatives of Israel and representatives of Jordan to be joined by the elected representatives of the inhabitants of the West Bank and Gaza, to negotiate a peace treaty between Israel and Jordan, taking into account the agreement reached on the final status of the West Bank and Gaza. The negotiations shall be based on all the provisions and principles of UN Security Council Resolution #242. The negotiations shall resolve, among other matters, the location of the boundaries and the nature of the security arrangements. The solution from the negotiations must also recognize the legitimate rights of the Palestinian people and their just requirements. In this way, the Palestinians will participate in the determination of their own future through:

1. The negotiations among Egypt, Israel, Jordan and the inhabitants of the West Bank and Gaza to agree on the final status of the West Bank and Gaza and other outstanding issues by the end of the transition period.
2. Submitting their agreement to a vote by the elected representatives of the inhabitants of the West Bank and Gaza.
3. Providing for the elected representatives of the inhabitants of the West Bank and Gaza to decide how they shall govern themselves consistent with the provisions of their agreement.
4. Participating as stated above in the work of the committee negotiating the peace treaty between Israel and Jordan.
5. All necessary measures will be taken and provisions made to assure the security of Israel and its neighbors during the transitional period and beyond. To assist in providing such security, a strong local police force will be constituted by the self-governing authority. It will be composed of inhabitants of the West Bank and Gaza. The police will maintain continuing liaison on internal security matters with the designated Israeli, Jordanian, and Egyptian officers.
6. During the transitional period, representatives of Egypt, Israel, and Jordan and the self-governing authority will constitute a continuing committee to decide by agreement on the modalities of admission of persons displaced from the West Bank and Gaza in 1967, together with necessary measures to prevent disruption and disorder. Other matters of common concern may also be dealt with by this committee.
7. Egypt and Israel will work with each other and with other interested parties to establish agreed procedures for a prompt, just, and permanent implementation of the resolution of the refugee problem.

B. Egypt — Israel

1. Egypt and Israel undertake not to resort to the threat or use of force to settle disputes. Any disputes shall be settled by peaceful means in accordance with the provisions of Article 33 of the charter of the United Nations.

2. In order to achieve peace between them, the parties agree to negotiate in good faith with a goal of concluding within three months from the signing of this framework a peace treaty between them, while inviting the other parties to the conflict to proceed simultaneously to negotiate and conclude similar peace treaties with a view to achieving a comprehensive peace in the area. The framework for the conclusion of a peace treaty between Egypt and Israel will govern the peace negotiations between them. The parties will agree on the modalities and the timetable for the implementation of their obligations under the treaty.

C. Associated Principles

Egypt and Israel state that the principles and provisions described below should apply to peace treaties between Israel and each of its neighbors — Egypt, Jordan, Syria and Lebanon.

Signatories shall establish among themselves relationships normal to states at peace with one another. To this end, they should undertake to abide by all the provisions of the Charter of the United Nations. Steps to be taken in this respect include:

    a. full recognition
    b. abolishing economic boycotts
    c. guaranteeing that under their jurisdiction, the citizens of the other parties shall enjoy the protection of the due process of law.

2. Signatories should explore possibilities for economic development in the context of final peace treaties, with the objective of contributing to the atmosphere of peace, cooperation and friendship which is their common goal.

3. Claims commissions may be established for the mutual settlement of all financial claims.

4. The United States shall be invited to participate in the talks on matters related to the modalities of the implementation of the agreements and working out the timetable for carrying out the obligations of the parties.
5. The United Nations Security Council shall be requested to endorse the peace treaties and ensure that their provisions shall not be violated. The permanent members of the Security Council shall be requested to underwrite the peace treaties and ensure respect for their provisions. They shall also be requested to conform their policies and actions with the undertakings contained in this framework.

For the government of the Arab Republic of Egypt
A. Sadat

For the government of Israel
M. Begin

Witnessed by:
Jimmy Carter, President of the United States of America.

FRAMEWORK FOR CONCLUDING A PEACE TREATY BETWEEN ISRAEL AND EGYPT

In order to achieve peace between them, Israel and Egypt agree to negotiate in good faith with a goal of concluding within three months of the signing of this Framework a peace treaty between them.
It is agreed that:
    The site of the negotiations will be under a United Nations flag at a location or locations to be mutually agreed.
    All of the principles of UN Resolution #242 will apply in this resolution of the dispute between Israel and Egypt.
    Unless otherwise mutually agreed, terms of the peace treaty will be implemented between two and three years after the peace treaty is signed.
    The following matters are agreed upon between the parties:

a. the full exercise of Egyptian sovereignty up to the internationally recognized border between Egypt and mandated Palestine;

b. the withdrawal of Israeli armed forces from the Sinai;

c. the use of airfields left by the Israelis near El Arish, Rafah, Ras en Naqb, and Sharm el Sheikh for civilian purposes only, including possible commercial use by all nations;

d. the right of free passage by ships of Israel through the Gulf of the Suez and the Suez Canal on the basis of the Constantinople Convention of 1888 applying to all nations; the Straight of Tiran and the Gulf of Aqaba are international waterways to be open to all nations for unimpeded and nonsuspendable freedom of navigation and overflight;

e. the construction of a highway between the Sinai and Jordan near Elat with guaranteed free and peaceful passage by Egypt and Jordan; and

f. the stationing of military forces listed below.

Stationing of Forces

A. No more than one division (mechanized or infantry) of Egyptian armed forces will be stationed within an area lying approximately 50 kilometers east of the Gulf of Suez and the Suez Canal.

B. Only United Nations forces and civilian police equipped with light weapons to perform normal police functions will be stationed within an area lying west of the international border and the Gulf of Aqaba, varying in width from 20 kilometers to 40 kilometers.

C. In the area within 3 kilometers east of the international border there will be Israeli limited military forces not to exceed four infantry battalions and United Nations observers.

D. Border patrol units, not to exceed three battalions, will supplement the civil police in maintaining order in the area not included above.

The exact demarcation of the above areas will be decided during the peace negotiations.

Early warning stations may exist to insure compliance with the terms of the agreement.

United Nations forces will be stationed: a. in part of the area in the Sinai lying within about 20 kilometers of the Mediterranean Sea and adjacent to the international border, and b. in the Sharm el Sheikh area to ensure freedom of passage through the Straight of Tiran; and these forces will not be removed unless such removal is approved by the Security Council of the United Nations with a unanimous vote of the five permanent members.

After a peace treaty is signed, and after the interim withdrawal is complete, normal relations will be established between Egypt and Israel, including: full recognition, including diplomatic, economic and cultural relations; termination of economic boycotts and barriers to the free movement of goods and people; and mutual protection of citizens by the due process of law.

Interim Withdrawal

Between three months and nine months after the signing of the peace treaty, all Israeli forces will withdraw east of a line extending from a point east of El Arish to Ras Muhamad, the exact location of this line to be determined by mutual agreement.

For the Government of the Arab Republic of Egypt
A. Sadat

For the Government of Israel
M. Begin

Witnessed by:
Jimmy Carter, President of the United States of America

UN SECURITY COUNCIL RESOLUTION #242

The Security Council, expressing its continuing concern with the grave situation in the Middle East, emphasizing the inadmissibility of the acquisiion of territory by war and the need to work for a just and lasting peace in which every State in the area can live in security,

emphasizing further that all member States in their acceptance of the Charter of the United Nations have undertaken a commitment to act in accordance with Article 2 of the Charter,

1. Affirms that the fulfillment of Charter principles requires the establishment of a just and lasting peace in the Middle East which should include the application of both the following principles:

    a. Withdrawal of Israeli armed forces from territories occupied in the recent conflict;

    b. Termination of all claims or states of belligerency and respect for and acknowledgement of the sovereignty, territorial integrity and political independence of every State in the area and their right to live in peace within secure and recognized boundaries free from threats or acts of force;

2. Affirms further the necessity:

    a. For guaranteeing freedom of navigation through international waterways in the area;

    b. For achieving a just settlement of the refugee problem;

    c. For guaranteeing the territorial inviolability and political independence of every State in the area, through measures including the establishment of demilitarized zones;

3. Requests the Secretary General to designate a Special Representative to proceed to the Middle East to establish and maintain contacts with the States concerned in order to promote agreement and assist efforts to achieve a peaceful and accepted settlement in accordance with the provisions and principles in this resolution;

4. Requests the Secretary General to report to the Security Council on the progress of the efforts of the Special Representative as soon as possible.

Adopted unanimously on November 22, 1967.

UN SECURITY COUNCIL RESOLUTION #338

The Security Council

1. Calls upon all parties to the present fighting to cease all firing and terminate all military activity immediately, no later than 12 hours after the moment of the adoption of this decision, in the positions they now occupy;

2. Calls upon the parties concerned to start immediately after the cease fire the implementation of Security Council Resolution # 242 (1967) in all of its parts;

3. Decides that, immediately and concurrently with the cease fire, negotiations start between the parties concerned under appropriate auspices aimed at establishing a just and durable peace in the Middle East.

Adopted on October 22, 1973, by a vote of 14 to 0
Resolution #338

Chapter 4

LETTERS LEADING TO THE CAMP DAVID ACCORDS

From Prime Minister Begin to President Carter
September 17, 1978
Subject: Sinai Settlements

Dear Mr. President:
I have the honor to inform you that during two weeks after my return home I will submit a motion before Israel's Parliament (the Knesset) to decide on the following question:

If during the negotiations to conclude a peace treaty between Israel and Egypt all outstanding issues are agreed upon, "Are you in favor of the removal of the Israeli settlers from the northern and southern Sinai areas, or are you in favor of keeping the aforementioned settlers in those areas?"

The vote, Mr. President, on this issue will be completely free from the usual Parliamentary Party discipline to the effect that although the coalition is being now supported by 70 members out of 120, every member of the Knesset, as I believe, both on the Government and the Opposition benches will be enabled to vote in accordance with his own conscience.

Sincerely Yours,

Signed
Menachem Begin

Camp David, Maryland:
From President Carter to President Sadat

Dear Mr. President Sadat:
I transmit herewith a copy of a letter to me from Prime Minister Begin setting forth how he proposes to present the issue of the Sinai settlements to the Knesset for the latter's decision.

In this connection, I understand from your letter that Knesset approval to withdraw all Israeli settlers from Sinai according to a timetable within the period specified for the implementation of the peace treaty is a prerequisite to any negotiations on a peace treaty between Egypt and Israel.

Sincerely,

Signed
Jimmy Carter

ENCLOSURE: Letter from Prime Minister Begin
Cairo: From President Sadat to President Carter
September 17, 1978

Dear Mr. President Carter:
In connection with the "Framework" for a settlement in Sinai to be signed tonight, I would like to reaffirm the position of the Arab Republic of Egypt with respect to the settlements:
1. All Israeli settlers must be withdrawn from Sinai according to a timetable within the period specified for the implementation of the peace treaty.
2. Agreement by the Israeli Government and its constitutional institutions to this basic principle is therfore a prerequisite to starting peace negotiations for concluding a peace treaty.
3. If Israel fails to meet this commitment, the "Framework" shall be void and invalid.

Sincerely,

Signed
Mohammed Anwar El Sadat

From President Carter to Prime Minister Begin

Dear Mr. Prime Minister Begin:
I have received your letter of September 17, 1978, describing how you intend to place the question of the future of Israeli settlements in Sinai before the Knesset for its decision.
    Enclosed is a copy of President Sadat's letter to me on this subject.

Sincerely,

Signed
Jimmy Carter

Jerusalem: From President Sadat to President Cater
September 17, 1978

Dear Mr. President Carter:
I am writing you to reaffirm the position of the Arab Republic of Egypt with respect to Jerusalem:

1. Arab Jerusalem is an integral part of the West Bank. Legal and historical Arab rights in the city must be respected and restored.

2. Arab Jerusalem should be under Arab Sovereignty.

3. The Palestinian inhabitants of Arab Jerusalem are entitled to exercise their legitimate national rights, being part of the Palestinian people in the West Bank.

4. Relevant Security Council Resolutions, particularly Resolutions #242 and #267, must be applied with regard to Jerusalem. All the measures taken by Israel to alter the status of the City are null and void and should be rescinded.

5. All peoples must have free access to the city and enjoy the free exercise of worship and the right to visit and transit to holy places without distinction or discrimination.

6. The holy places of each faith may be placed under the administration and control of their representatives.

7. Essential functions in the city should be undivided and a joint municipal council composed of an equal number of Arab and Israeli members can supervise the carrying out of these functions. In this way, the city shall be undivided.

Sincerely,

Signed
Mohammed Anwar El Sadat

From Prime Minister Begin to President Carter
September 17, 1978

Dear Mr. President Carter:
I have the honor to inform you, Mr. President, that on the 28 June 1967, Israel's Parliament (the Knesset) promulgated and adopted a law to the effect: "The Government is empowered by a decree to apply the law, the jurisdiction and administration of the State to any part of Eretz Israel (land of Israel-Palestine), as stated in that decree."

On that basis of this law, the Government of Israel decreed in July, 1967, that Jerusalem is one city indivisible, the Capital of the State of Israel.

Sincerely,

Signed
Menachem Begin

Camp David, Maryland:
From President Carter to President Sadat

Dear Mr. President Sadat:
I have received your letter of September 17, 1978, setting forth the Egyptian position on Jerusalem. I am transmitting a copy of that letter to Prime Minister Begin for his information.

The position of the United States on Jerusalem remains as stated by Ambassador Goldberg in the United Nations General Assembly on July 14, 1967, and subsequently by Ambassador Yost in the United Nations Security Council on July 1, 1969.

Sincerely,

Signed
Jimmy Carter

Cairo: From President Sadat to President Carter
September 17, 1978
Subject: Implementation of Comprehensive Settlement

Dear Mr. President Carter:
In connection with the "Framework for Peace in the Middle East," I am writing you this letter to inform you of the position of the Arab Republic of Egypt, with respect to implementation of the comprehensive settlement.

To insure the implementation of the provisions related to the West Bank and Gaza and in order to safeguard the legitimate rights of the Palestinian people, Egypt will be prepared to assume the Arab role emanating from these provisions, following consultations with Jordan and the representatives of the Palestinian people.

Sincerely,

Signed
Mohammed Anwar El Sadat

Washington D.C.: From President Carter to
Prime Minister Begin
September 22, 1978
Subject: Definition of Terms

Dear Mr. Prime Minister Begin:
I hereby acknowledge that you have informed me as follows:
A. In each paragraph of the agreed Framework Document the expressions "Palestinians," or Palestinian People, are being and will be construed and understood by you, as "Palestinian Arabs."
B. In each paragraph in which the expression "West Bank" appears, it is being and will be understood by the Government of Israel as Judea and Samaria.

               Sincerely,

                 Signed
               Jimmy Carter

Washington D.C.: From U.S. Secretary of Defense to
Prime Minister Begin
September 28, 1978
Subject: Airbases

Dear Mr. Minister:
The U.S. understands that, in connection with carrying out the agreements reached at Camp David, Israel intends to build two military airbases at appropriate sites in the Negev to replace the airbases at Eitam and Etzion which will be evacuated by Israel in accordance with the peace treaty to be concluded between Egypt and Israel. We also understand the special urgency and priority which Israel attaches to preparing the new bases in light of its conviction that it cannot safely leave the Sinai airbases until the new ones are operational.

 I suggest that our two governments consult on the scope and costs of the two new airbases as well as on related forms of assistance which the United States might appropriately provide in light of the special problems which may be presented by carrying out such a project on an urgent basis. The President is prepared to seek the necessary Congressional approvals for such assistance as may be agreed upon by the U.S. side as a result of such consultations.

Signed
Harold Brown
Secretary of Defense

The Honorable — Ezer Weizman
Minister of Defense
Government of Israel

Chapter 5

EVENTS FOLLOWING THE CAMP DAVID ACCORDS

September, 1978

9-18-78
Begin denies Israel will halt buildup of West Bank outposts.
Washington, D.C.

Cracks began to appear today in the fragile structure of Mid-East peace fashioned at Camp David, as Egyptian Foreign Minister Mohammed Kamel resigned and Israeli Prime Minister Menachem Begin differed with U.S. officials about Israel's right to put new settlements on the West Bank.

Reports of Kamel's resignation were confirmed by knowledgeable American officials, who expressed fear it was an indication that Egyptian President Anwar Sadat could not sell the agreement to the Arab world.

Kamel became Foreign Minister after Ismail Fahmy resigned last year in protest of Sadat's initial peace overture to Israel.

Begin, speaking in Hebrew to an audience limited to Israeli reporters, cast more doubt on the durability of the agreement when he said Israel had made no commitment to refrain from establishing new settlements on the West

Bank during the five-year transition period envisaged by the agreement.

After Begin, Sadat, and President Carter signed the agreement yesterday, American officials told reporters that Israel had committed itself to establishing no new settlements during the negotiations for Palestinian autonomy in the region.

Begin reported that Israel planned to maintain a military presence in the West Bank to ensure Israeli security.

Sadat met separately this morning at the Egyptian embassy with Vice-President Walter Mondale of the United States, former Secretary of State Henry Kissinger, and former Vice-President Nelson Rockefeller.

Although the Congress has no direct role in implementation of the agreements, Carter and his summit partners are seeking moral support for their efforts.

The dramatic proposal for an Egyptian-Israeli treaty may not sit well with Egypt's Arab neighbors because it would involve a separate peace that would leave unsettled the conflict with Jordan, Syria, and Lebanon.

In sketching one of the key agreements, President Carter said Israel would end its military rule of the West Bank of the Jordan River over a five-year period, while retaining some military outposts.

The Palestinian Arabs now living under Israeli occupation there and in the Gaza Strip would choose their own "self-governing" authority and participate in negotiations to determine their future.

A major question left unresolved was whether concessions offered by Israel to the Palestinian Arabs will draw Jordan's King Hussein into the peace process.

9-19-78
Israel will not give up its sovereignity
Washington, D.C.

Prime Minister Menachem Begin told Congress that Israel has no intention of giving up its claim to sovereignty or its right to station troops in disputed areas of the West Bank and the Gaza Strip.

Begin told leaders of the House in a breakfast meeting that they should not misinterpret the Camp David Accords to mean that Israel has committed itself to restoring Arab sovereignty to those lands, which it captured in the 1967 War.

Meanwhile, Secretary of State Cyrus Vance added Syrian President Hafez Assad to the list of Arab leaders he will visit to explain the Camp David agreements and seek support for them. He previously had scheduled stops in Jordan and Saudi Arabia on a trip in which he departs tonight.

Sadat told members of the Senate Foreign Relations Committee he believes Jordan and Saudi Arabia eventually will support the Middle East agreements. The President of Egypt said, "Whenever there is any agreement that will permit the establishment of peace so that no one encroaches on the other's land or sovereignty, then all Arabs will be behind it."

Prime Minister Begin stated, "I believe with all my heart that the Jewish people have a right to sovereignty over Judea, Samaria, and the Gaza Strip to have peace," using biblical names for the lands on the West Bank. The Bible gives us that right.

The Camp David Accord calls for the replacement of Israel's military government with an autonomous government, elected by the Palestinians who live there. Israel's troops would be garrisoned in specified locations.

Secretary of State Cyrus Vance will spend two nights in Amman, Jordan to confer with King Hussein, then fly to Riyadh, Saudi Arabia, to see King Khaled.

After an overnight stop, he will spend five hours in Damascus with Assad, returning to Washington D.C. to brief President Carter.

In talking with Assad, Vance will try to draw the Syrian leader away from the "rejectionists" — the Arab countries opposing any reconciliation with Israel — and bring him into the Middle East negotiating process.

Assad has been sharply critical of Sadat's approaches to Israel and had broken his alliance with Sadat after the Egyptian leader's trip to Jerusalem. Syria reached an interim agreement with Israel recovering some territory on the Golan Heights in 1975. The support of both nations is considered vital to the outcome of the "Framework for Peace" that Sadat, Begin, and Carter signed at Camp David.

The other immediate concern was the status of Israel settlements in occupied Egyptian territory. The issue was unresolved at Camp David with Sadat insisting that the settlements be removed as a condition to any Israeli-Egyptian peace treaty. Begin refused to agree to such a step, but said he would leave the final decision to the Israeli parliament.

9-20-78
Vance in Mid-East to sell Accords
Amman, Jordan

Secretary of State Cyrus Vance arrived here today on the first leg of a Mid-East trip designed to keep Jordan and Saudi Arabia out of an Arab front bent on derailing the Camp David Accord. He also hoped to ease Syria's opposition to the agreements.

Vance was scheduled to meet with four Arab leaders — King Hussein of Jordan, King Khaled and Crown Prince Fahd of Saudi Arabia in Riyadh within two days, and President Hafez Assad of Syria in Damascus the following day.

Meanwhile, there were these developements relating to the Camp David summit and the Mid-East.

President Carter and Israeli Prime Minister Begin agreed during the summit that after establishing a framework for peace, no new Israeli settlements would be started for a period of three months.

American, Israeli, and Egyptian leaders are distinctly cool to the idea of basing any U.S. military forces in the Middle East.

Vance said he would explain to the "key Arab" governments represented at Camp David the contents, purpose, and philosophy of the understandings reached, so they can make their own decisions on how to respond to the invitations to them contained in the basic documents.

The Secretary's mission was set back at the start by statements from Jordan saying it would not be bound by the agreements and from Saudi Arabia stating they could not be considered as an acceptable final formula for peace.

Both Jordan and Saudi Arabia reiterated the primary Arab demand for Israeli withdrawal from all territory occupied in the 1967 War, including East Jerusalem, which the Camp David Accords do not guarantee.

Both called for unification of Arab policy.

One factor for acceptance is the cultivation of the Saudis as exemplified by the sale of F-15 fighter jets from the United States. Another is the conservatism of the oil rich Saudi monarchy.

9-21-78
Vance in Arabia after striking out in Jordan
Riyadh, Saudi Arabia

Secretary of State Cyrus Vance failed to win Jordan's backing for the Camp David Accords and flew to Saudi Arabia to seek the powerful kingdom's help in the U.S. mediated peace plan.

In seeking their support, Vance will remind the Saudis of the Carter administration plan to sell F-15 fighter planes to their country.

Jordanian Foreign Minister Hassain Ibrahim, standing with Vance at Amman airport, said Jordan still has reservations about the Camp David Accord's failure to deal with the question of ultimate status of the Israeli-occupied West Bank and the Palestinian people.

In the meetings with King Hussein, the Americans received a commitment for a continuing dialogue with Jordan on its critical role in the peace process.

The Saudi influence derives from several sources. As custodians of the holiest shrines of Islam, they are important religious leaders. As the Middle East's largest oil producer and the owners of the world's largest proven oil reserves, they subsidize Syria, Egypt, Jordan, and other poorer Arab states.

Saudi Arabia cannot be considered a final acceptable formula for peace because they do not guarantee Israel withdrawal from all occupied territory, including East Jerusalem, the Palestinian right to self-determination and their own state, and recognition of the Palestine Liberation Organization as the sole, legitimate representative of the Palestinian people.

9-23-78
Begin cheered at home
Tel Aviv, Israel

Welcomed by chanting, cheering thousands tossing flowers and waving banners, Prime Minister Menachem Begin came home, saying he brought a peace agreement with security and honor from the Camp David Mid-East summit.
"We are proud of you," said the happy enthusiasts. "Peace with Egypt in our time."
"We brought you a peace agreement from Camp David with security and Honor," Begin told members of his government and the opposition who assembled on the tarmac (road surface around a airfield) to greet him. There are problems which we have yet to overcome. Hard days are ahead of us. There will be tests and trials.
In Cairo, Egyptians prepared a similar hero's welcome for President Anwar Sadat. Colored lights decorated shops and streets, and colorful banners proclaimed him a "hero of peace" and implored "God's blessing on the wise leader of Egypt."
Begin praised the Israeli negotiators at Camp David as a "true team" and thanked President Carter for his many hours of effort during the talks.

The Prime Minister of Israel stated that President Sadat of Egypt and the Egyptian negotiators "made the contribution on the last day so that we could say Yes, we do have an agreement, the foundation for peace."

9-23-78
Sadat returns home to acclamation of his people
Cairo, Egypt

A joyous crowd met President Anwar Sadat at the Cairo airport to greet the Egyptian leader. President Carter, Prime Minister Menachem Begin, and President Sadat had formulated and signed the Camp David Accords calling for an elected Arab government and a five-year transition period for the West Bank and Gaza.

Sadat said he would consult with Jordan and the Palestinian people, but left open the possibility proceeding to the negotiating table without their formal consent.

Jordan's King Hussein rejected a personal appeal by Arab hard-liners Moammar Khadafy of Libya and Palestinian Yasser Arafat to join the anti-Camp David Bloc.

"The King will not respond to any appeals or pressures and his moderate stance remains the same," a Jordanian government official said after Hussein conferred with his longtime adversaries Khadafy and Arafat in an unusual meeting at a secluded Jordanian air base.

It is too soon to speculate about Sadat's offer, or even whether Sadat will face a decision of "going it alone," but the prospect has some appealing advantages for many of those involved.

Sadat would be free to conclude a peace treaty with Israel and regain the Sinai, while preserving his insistence that he is not imperiling the Palestinian Arabs living in Israeli occupied territory.

Israel would have a new Palestinian entity with which to negotiate. An elected civil authority would be far less hostile than the Palestinian Liberation Organization, dedicated to the destruction of the Jewish State and which has wide Arab recognition as the sole voice of the Palestinians. Hussein would gain a painless way to wait and watch developments before deciding whether to turn his back on the militants and join talks with Israel.

9-24-78
Sadat hailed
Cairo, Egypt

More than 100,000 cheering Egyptians welcomed President Anwar Sadat home while in Damascus, Syria, and Iraq. Other Arab leaders put the final touches on a "rejectionist" plan to undermine the Camp David Accords.
    Syrian President Hafez Assad, addressing the closing session of the Damascus conference, said it had been "very fruitful" in countering the agreements at Camp David, which he called "the summit of surrender."
    In a public communique, the anti-Sadat leaders agreed to form a military pact of Syria, Algeria, Libya, South Yemen, and the Palestinian Liberation Organization, observe an economic boycott of Egypt, develop closer relations with the Soviet Union, and demand that Arab League headquarters be moved from Cairo.
    Some of the militants, such as George Habash of the popular Front for the Liberation of Palestine, have threatened to launch guerilla operations against U.S. interests in the Mid-East and elsewhere.
    President Carter of the United States at a meeting in Pittsburgh, Pennsylvania, stated that unless the Palestinians and Jordan's King Hussein join the Mid-East talks, "the progress will be limited."
    In other developments in Jordan, King Hussein repeated his countries' objections to the U.S. engineered peace proposals and chastized Sadat for suggesting that Egypt might "go it alone" and negotiate an agreement with Israel over the West Bank without Jordanian participation in the peace talks.

9-25-78
Vance back: no peace gains.
Washington D.C.

Secretary of State Cyrus Vance returned home today, conceding that his five-day Mid-East trip had produced no tangible results in President Carter's bid to gain Arab support for the Camp David Accords.
That assessment was a far cry from the ringing send-off he received from a cheering joint session of Congress the previous week.
Vance's final stop in Damascus where he met with Syrian President Hafez Assad gave the Secretary no encouragement. Assad has called the Accords "treasonous," because they do not guarantee complete Israeli withdrawal.

9-28-78
Israel O.K.'s pact, maps Egypt talks.
Jerusalem

The Israeli government began preparations today for peace negotiations with Egypt, its largest Arabian foe, after the Israeli Parliament voted by an overwhelming margin to ratify the camp David Accords and withdraw all Jewish settlers from the Sinai Peninsula if Egypt makes peace.
Prime Minister Menachem Begin said negotiations could start as early as next week on the peace treaty which he and President Anwar Sadat pledged at Camp David to complete within three months.
Egypt's acting foreign minister, Butros Ghali, replied in Cairo that Israeli and Egyptian delegations would meet either in Ismalia, on the Suez Canal, or in El Arish, the Sinai capital.
An advanced Israeli party was going to Cairo today to re-establish the direct links Egyptian President Anwar Sadat severed in July.

Ghali, speaking with reporters, lauded the Knesset decision as "proof of a positive change in Israeli public opinion because they now realize that occupying other countries' lands cannot bring peace."

He also urged other Arab nations to reconsider their refusal to negotiate with Israel, so that "we can achieve a comprehensive peace in the region."

The 120 members of the Knesset, Israel's one-house parliament, put peace with Egypt in exchange for the Sinai settlements to a vote following more than 17 hours of emotional debate. The vote of 84-19 with 17 abstentions showed wide acceptance for the two frameworks for peace drafted at Camp David and the painful settlement resolution demanded as a condition for further negotiations by Sadat.

Winding up the debate, Begin stated a peace treaty between Israel and Egypt would be "the great turning point in the history of the Middle East."

President Carter hailed the Knesset vote as a "great step forward" and sure proof of the courage of Prime Minister Begin and the Knesset. In other developments:

U.S. Mid-East envoy Alfred Atherton left Jordan for Israel after briefing King Hussein on Secretary of State Cyrus Vance's talks with Saudi Arabian and Syrian leaders last week. Vance had met with Hussein before going to Saudi Arabia and Syria. Hussein had refused to endorse the Camp David Accords.

Syrian President Hafez Assad met with Kuwati leaders in that oil-rich area to explain his rejection of the accords. Syrian sources said Assad and Kuwait's ruler, Emir Sheikh Jaber Al-Ahmad as Sabah, agreed the U.S. - inspired accords could not serve as the basis for a comprehensive Mid-East peace.

October, 1978

10-2-78
Renewed talks on peace treaty
Washington, D.C.

Negotiations to complete the Egyptian-Israeli peace treaty, outlined in the Camp David summit accords last month, are reported to begin in Washington on October 12, 1978.

Egyptian President Anwar Sadat said today that President Carter will go to Cairo for the signing of the treaty.

The White House Secretary, Jody Powell, stated that final plans have not been made, but Israel and Egypt leaders have informally agreed to the conference. United States will be a full participant in the negotiations, which will be conducted at the ministerial level instead of by heads of state.

Egyptian government sources confirmed reports in Israel and Cairo that Washington had been chosen as the site for the talks rather than the location proposed by Egypt, the Suez Canal city of Ismalia. The shift would facilitate participation by American officials in the negotiations to end formally 30 years of hostilities between Egypt and Israel.

The Israeli parliament removed the last barrier to further peace talks when it agreed to President Anwar Sadat's demand that Israel withdraw it 4000 Jewish settlers from 18 outposts it established in the Sinai Desert.

In Cairo, Sadat made the announcement of the Carter conference while addressing his parliament on the Camp David Accords.

"President Carter will go down in history as one of the greatest leaders who changed the face of history from bitterness to love, and from war to peace," Sadat replied, adding the negotiations could not have succeeded without Carter's "perseverance."

10-14-78
Mid-East pact seen by next month
Washington D.C.

Cyrus Vance stated to reporters that Israel and Egypt may be able to conclude their peace treaty by Nobember 19, 1978, the first anniversary of President Anwar Sadat's visit to Jerusalem.

The Framework devised at Camp David called for completion of a treaty within 90 days - by December 17, but the Secretary of State, pleased with the course of the negotiations being held at Blair House, across the street from the White House, said it probably won't take that long.

Sources close to the talks said they were proceeding smoothly, reflecting a desire by the two longtime antagonists to come to terms quickly.

The negotiations are designed to determine the pace of Israeli withdrawal from the Sinai, which is being returned to Egyptian sovereignty, and security measures on that front.

November, 1978

11-3-78
Tel Aviv, Israel:

Defense Minister Ezer Weizman, returning today to report to the Cabinet on the Israeli-Egyptian peace talks, said Israel and Egypt have agreed to phase out the surveillance stationed in the Sinai Peninsula.

Weizman told reporters at Ben-Gurion Airport that military aspects of the draft treaty will form the major part of the report he will make to Prime Minister Menachem Begin's cabinet on Sunday. He said he expected to return to the United States on Monday.

Asked about reports in the Israeli press that the negotiators in Washington had agreed not to set up early warning systems in the Sinai, Weizman replied, "That's true. This particular detail is known and accepted by the cabinet."

Questioned about the American stations in the Sinai's Gidi and Mitla passes, Weizman said there would be no American stations.

Without further elaboration, Weizman thus signaled the end of the three surveillance stations — Israeli, Egyptian, and American — which have been standing within a few miles of each other for three years in the middle of the U.N. buffer zone.

Weizman said it was possible that this trip might mark the last time that a member of the Israeli delegation in Washington would have to return to get new authorization from the cabinet.

11-4-78
Vance sees gains in the Mid-East Talks
Washington, D.C.

Almost all obstacles to a peace treaty between Egypt and Israel have been cleared away as the two sides continue to make "steady progress" toward agreement, Secretary of State Cyrus R. Vance said Friday.

Reporting at a news conference on his 2½-hour meeting Thursday with Israeli Prime Minister Menachem Begin, Vance said a key objective now is to begin negotiations over the future of Gaza and the West Bank of the Jordan River.

Vance's optimistic assessment of the course of the Egyptian-Israel peace talks appeared to bolster reports that the treaty could be completed within a week to 10 days.

We have now resolved almost all the substantive issues, he said. Vance said most of his discussion with Begin concerned how to begin a second round of negotiations over the West Bank and Gaza under a Framework established in September at Camp David, Maryland.

The Framework set by President Carter, Begin, and Egyptian President Anwar Sadat provided for four-way negotiations involving Jordan and the Palestinians have not indicated a willingness to participate.

Vance confirmed that he and Begin discussed U.S. assistance to Israel, in the form of a loan, to finance the Israeli withdrawal from the Sinai. Sources said the amount discussed was $3.75 billion.

11-5-78
Sadat rejects billions to halt separate peace
Baghdad, Iraq

Leaders of 20 Arab nations sent a delegation to Cairo Saturday in a last-ditch bid to talk Anwar Sadat out of making a separate peace with Israel, but the Egyptian President responded with a swift and angry rebuff.

The four-man delegation carried with it an implicit offer of massive Arab financial aid if Egypt abandons its go-it-alone peace drive. But Sadat declared to the Egyptian Parliament, "All the millions in the world will not buy the will of Egypt."

The reconciliation mission dispatched by the Arab summit meeting here was headed by Lebanese Prime Minister Salim Hoss.

Sadat went before the Parliament in Cairo a short time after word reached the Egyptian capital that the Hoss group was headed there.

Before coming to this rostrum, he told the legislators, "We were informed by foreign news agencies that those meeting in Baghdad had sent a delegation which was already on its way. They did not ask permission. They shall not meet with me or any Egyptian official."

Sadat told a news conference later, however, that he would be willing to meet with Arab heads of state.

"If they choose to come to Egypt, they are welcome and I am ready to sit with them and discuss everything."

The official Iraqian news agency said Hoss delegation carried a message from President Ahmed Hassan Bakr of Iraq, chairman of the Arab League summit, saying that if Sadat agreed to return to the Arab fold, "the summit conference promises to guarantee the steadfastness of Egypt and its people."

That was a clear reference to an Iraqian proposal at the conference that the Arab countries give Egypt up to $5 billion to draw Sadat away from his growing dependence on the West for bolstering his sagging economy.

The delegation was instructed to deliver the message, report on the results of the summit so far, and receive the

Egyptian leader's reply before returning to Baghdad. They were met by only a junior official at the Cairo airport.

With Hoss were Syrian information Minister Ahmed Iskandar, Iraqian Baath Party official Tariq Aziz, and Foreign Minister Ahmed Suedy of the United Arab Emirates. Hoss and Suedy represent governments with relatively moderate positions on Egypt's peace moves. Syria and Iraq are leading hard-line states in the opposition to the U.S. - sponsored Egyptian-Israeli negotiations.

Egypt was the only member of the 21-nation Arab League not represented at the summit, which was called by Iraq specifically to reach a united Arab stand against the bilateral peace. It appeared the participants in the Baghdad meeting probably would not reach a concensus on how to react to the impending peace treaty.

11-9-78
Egypt — Israel accords link to Mid-East peace sought by President
Kansas City, Missouri

President Carter said today he believes any peace agreement between Egypt and Israel should be linked to negotiations for an overall Middle East settlement, particularly the status of Palestinians on the Jordan River.

Carter's statement during a nationally broadcast news conference placed him in agreement with the stand of President Anwar Sadat of Egypt; Prime Minister Menachem Begin of Israel has sought to separate the agreement being neogtiated in Washington from other Middle East issues.

President Carter said that a commitment for an overall Middle East settlement was part of the outline for peace reached at Camp David.

One of the premises for the Camp David negotiations was a comprehensive peace settlement, the President said.

11-26-78
Egypt to ask for new talks
Cairo, Egypt

Some time has elapsed since the last editorial. There is serious disagreement between Israel and Egypt on the comprehensive peace settlement. Egypt will ask President Carter to seek a resumption of the Mid-East peace talks with Israel, Prime Minister Mustafa Khalil said yesterday.

He said Egypt considers Israel's "take-it-or-leave-it approach to the U.S. draft treaty sumbitted to Cairo and Tel Aviv as an ultimatum," such an "intransigent attitude does not serve the cause of peace at all," Khalil said.

Earlier, Egyptian President hinted that he may not go to Norway an December 10, 1978 to accept the Nobel Peace Prize he won jointly with Prime Minister Menachem Begin unless the impasse in the Washington peace negotiations is broken.

The Cairo newspaper *Al Ahram* reported today that Egypt plans to reassert its efforts to achieve a treaty provision ensuring self-rule for Palestinians.

The Egyptian-Israeli peace talks bogged down when Israel refused to accept an Egyptian demand for a timetable on giving autonomy to Palestinians on the West Bank of the Jordan River in the Gaza Strip.

Khalil said that if Israel refuses to join in another round of talks "they would be breaking the negotiations."

Egypt seeks a modification in a clause in the U.S. draft that Khalil said would bar Egypt from committing itself to any arrangements — military or economic — with other Arab countries.

Israel has argued that the planned treaty must supersede Egypt's agreements with Arab states such as mutual defense pacts and economic boycott regulations directed against the Jewish state.

Khalil said the lack of agreement over "specific steps" for Palestinian autonomy raises the eventuality of dispute and thereby does not settle the 30-year-old Mid-East conflict.

December, 1978

12-8-78

Israeli Foreign Minister Moshe Dayan said today he disagreed with President Carter that Israel and Egypt must sign a peace treaty by the December 17, 1978 deadline set at the Camp David summit.

"I cannot share this attitude," Dayan told a news conference in Bern, Switzerland.

"If we sign by then, so much the better, but with an issue like peace negotiation with an Arab country with whom we have had 30 years of war, I would not say we should shut the door and say sorry after December 17."

Dayan talked to reporters before boarding a flight to Tel Aviv after a three-day official visit to Switzerland.

He also ruled out a meeting in Europe with Prime Minister Mustapha Khalil, who is in Paris, France. "I am going home now and will not be meeting with any Egyptian officials," Dayan said.

Carter expressed grave concern that failure to meet the December 17 deadline would cast doubt on the intentions of President Anwar Sadat of Egypt and Israeli Prime Minister Menachem Begin to carry out other aspects of the agreement.

12-10-78
U.S. may pull out of peace talks
Memphis, Tennessee

The Israelis and the Egyptians would be well advised to heed President Carter's warning that their failure to sign a formal peace treaty by December 17, 1978, only seven days from today, would kill the great hopes for Middle East peace raised at Camp David last September.

Carter, who has made plain his growing irritation over delaying tactics by both sides during the past three months, told reporters at the White House breakfast meeting that he would consider the Camp David accords abrogated if the

December 17 deadline set for the signing of a formal peace treaty between Egypt and Israel is not met.
During the course of all of the Egyptian-Israeli jockeying for an advantage, Sadat and Begin have indicated they did not feel bound by the December 17 deadline. Apparently they feel that President Carter, as the chief architect of the Camp David accords, would go along with them as long as necessary rather than risk a breakdown in the peace process.
The President is tired of being the man in the middle, subjected to whipsawing by both sides by the issue of autonomy for the Palestinians of Gaza and the West Bank of the Jordan River.

12-12-78
Vance meets Begin after Sadat parley
Jerusalem

Secretary of State Cyrus R. Vance and Prime Minister Menachem Begin met today to discuss fresh revisions in the U.S. draft of an Egyptian-Israeli peace treaty, while Egyptian President Anwar Sadat declared he was "quite ready" to sign the pact.
Vance shuttled to Israel to relay Egypt's conditional acceptance of a peace treaty, hammered out in meetings between the Egyptian leader and the U.S. envoy earlier this week, provided the treaty is linked to a commitment for elections among the Palestinians in the Israeli occupied Gaza strip.
"For our part we are quite ready. It depends on the other part," said Sadat in his first public comment on the peace moves since his meetings with Vance.
Sadat, appearing quite jovial, spoke with reporters in Cairo after receiving the Nobel Peace Prize medal from an aide who had accepted it for the President in Oslo, Norway on 12-10-78.
From the Israeli side, there was no immediate indication whether the modifications produced a breakthrough that

will get the stalled negotiations moving.

U.S. spokesman George Sherman, who briefed reporters, refused to characterize the discussion of the proposals.

"I don't like to give temperature readings, particularly at a preliminary session," Sherman said. "We do feel negotiations are at a delicate stage."

For the first time, informed sources said, Sadat gave the United States his approval of peace terms negotiated after the Camp David summit. But he made his acceptance conditional on Israel's agreeing to a commitment to hold elections among the 450,000 Palestinian Arabs living in the Gaza Strip.

So far, Begin has resisted linking Israeli-Egyptian peace in any way of autonomy to the Palestinians of Gaza and the West Bank of the Jordan River. The new U.S.-Egyptian formula is designed to gain Begin's acceptance to a partial linkage, in Gaza alone.

Palestinians in both areas have rejected the autonomy proposal so far, because it does not promise them a Palestinian state.

12-13-78
Vance reports snags in Mid-East parleys
Jerusalem

New snags late today clouded prospects for an Egyptian-Israeli peace treaty and Secretary of State Cyrus R. Vance accelerated plans to end his mission to the Middle East.

The decision to return for what a U.S. spokesman called "urgent business" was announced after Vance held two meetings with Israeli officials and talked to President Carter in Washington by telephone.

Earlier Vance had indicated he had high hopes for his session in Israel. He told reproters on his arrival from Cairo that he believed he was in the "final stages" of his Mid-East shuttle.

Sadat had also expressed optimism, saying he thought he was "quite ready" to sign a peace pact with Israel.

12-14-78
Vance fails to get approval on Egyptian demands
Jerusalem

Secretary of State Cyrus Vance failed to win Prime Minister Menachem Begin's agreement today to Egyptian peace treaty demands favored by the United States.

Vance prepared to return to Cairo and Washington a day ahead of schedule, and Begin called a special meeting of the Israeli cabinet to determine the government's course of action.

Vance after a final meeting with Begin said peace was still the "common goal" of the United States and Israel, "and we are determined that goal will be achieved."

The Israeli state radio said Prime Minister Begin found the Egyptian proposals unacceptable. Other Israeli sources claimed Egypt had hardened its negotiating position.

Reliable Israeli sources said Egypt had made three new demands, including some of it raised earlier and then dropped. They are:

1. The Egyptians want to delay the exchange of ambassadors between Cairo and Jerusalem until self-governing Palestinian councils are functioning on the West Bank of the Jordan River and in the Gaza Strip. A clause agreed on at Camp David last September calls for an exchange of ambassadors nine months after the treaty is signed.

2. Egypt wants an automatic review of the treaty's provisions after a specified period. Israel is opposed to such a review after it returns the Sinai Peninsula to Egypt.

3. Egypt wants to change a treaty provision designed to prevent Egypt from aiding other Arab states if they make war on Israel. The Egyptians reportedly want a letter attached to the treaty saying the provision would become effective only after a settlement between Israel and its other Arab adversaries, Jordan and Syria.

12-16-78
Israel rejects Egypt's new peace plans
Jerusalem

The Israeli cabinet today rejected Egypt's new peace demands, and Prime Minister Menachem Begin accused the United States of taking a "one-sided attitude" as a Mid-East mediator.

Begin declared Egypt bears "total responsibility" for failure to reach agreement on a treaty by the target date of December 17.

Begin spoke to reporters after a 4-hour special cabinet session that ended with unanimous support for the Prime Minister, who already had turned down the U.S. backed Egyptian ideas.

Begin said he had not lost faith in the American ability to be an "honest broker." The new conditions proposed by President Sadat that are unacceptable to Israel are as follows:

1. That an exchange of ambassadors be conditional on working out a plan for Palestinian self-rule, at least in the Gaza Strip.

2. That the treaty article on security arrangements in the Sinai Peninsula be altered to call for an automatic review after 5 years.

3. That a letter be appended to the treaty that would negate the "content of an article" saying the treaty supersedes previous agreements, such as Egypt's military obligations to other Arab states.

4. That there be a letter setting December, 1979, as a target date for electing a Palestinian council to govern the West Bank of the Jordan River and Gaza in place of Israel's military government.

Begin said a letter on the target date "can be clarified and be reformulated" but Israel still opposes any deadline or timetables.

The Israelis oppose linking the treaty with the Palestinian issue in these ways, contending that the deadline would give the Egyptians a pretext for voiding the treaty if there were unavoidable delays.

The Americans credited President Sadat for dropping his insistence on a step-by-step timetable for Palestinian autonomy, and for his willingness to transfer Egyptian demands from the treaty itself to letters attached to the treaty as annexes.

12-18-78
Mid-East deadline passed

The deadline set at Camp David for peace between Egypt and Israel passed uneventfully Sunday, the bright promise of September now dimmed, though not dead.

"You know today we should be on Mount Sinai," a jovial Anwar Sadat told a photographer at his presidential villa on the Nile River. The Egyptian President wants to sign a peace treaty with Israel on the historic mountain.

Asked when the current impasse in negotiations might end, Sadat said, "I don't know. It all depends on the Prime Minister's attitude."

One senior official from Israel, who asked not to be identified, told reporters in Jerusalem the negotiations "are not dead," but it would take a reconsideration by Egypt to get them moving again.

12-26-78
Israelis trying to abort Mid-East peace — Sadat
Cairo, Egypt

President Anwar Sadat said that Prime Minister Menachem Begin has "expansionist dreams" in the Middle East and that the Israelis are trying to "abort" peace in the region.

In a taped television interview marking his 60th birthday, Sadat declared that Begin wants to extend

"Israel's territory to the river Euphrates in the east and the river Nile in the southwest."

The Egyptian leader vowed not to permit conditions to return to the phase of no peace, no war in the region.

He also blamed radical Arab regimes for the stalemate in the Israeli-Egyptian peace talks in Washington. He said his Arab foes have encouraged Israel.

"I can't help wondering, when we managed to push Israel into the tight corner of peace, we were surprised to see some Arab regimes trying to refuel Israel's intransigence and give it reason to procrastinate and pursue expansionist dreams," Sadat said.

He said some Arab leaders still use outdated slogans such as, "throw Israel into the sea," and, "no negotiations and no peace" with Israel.

12-27-78
Begin says Israel ready to talk on treaty snags.
Jerusalem

Prime Minister Menachem Begin said Israel is ready to hold "clarification talks" on two snags still blocking a peace treaty with Egypt.

Following a meeting with his cabinet, he said his government would reconsider arrangements for Palestinian autonomy in the occupied territory and Egyptian military deployment in the Sinai Peninsula.

Begin said Israel would stand firm in its rejection of what he called "basic issues" proposed by Egypt and supported by the United States.

Although Israel would agree to reexamine the article in a draft treaty outlining military arrangements in the Sinai, it will not accept Egypt's demand for an automatic review after 5 years. A peace treaty is forever.

Reviewing the other points of the dispute, Begin said:

The treaty should stand on its own and not be dependent on the participation of Jordan or the Palestinians in a later series of talks.

Egypt's insistence on an explicit statement that its defense pacts with other Arab states remain valid is "a strange demand."

The exchange of resident ambassadors must not be linked to the establishment of autonomy in the occupied Gaza Strip.

Begin convened his top ministers earlier for a secret session attended by army officers with maps before the full cabinet met.

The peace negotiations broke down in mid-November, principally over the issue of a timetable linking Palestinian autonomy to the proposed bilateral peace treaty.

Egypt wants to ensure that a peace treaty with the Jewish State does not supersede its defense pacts with Arab nations.

Several Israeli cabinet ministers have privately criticized Dayan, spokesman for the Israelis, for saying, "I think it is possible to bridge the gap if both sides are willing to compromise or meet each other half way."

12-30-78
Begin vows West Bank expansion
Jerusalem

Prime Minister Menachem Begin pledged that new Jewish settlements will be built in the occupied West Bank of Jordan, but said the Israeli government had taken no decision yet on when or where.

Begin said he backed his foreign minister, Moshe Dayan, who spoke last week of a need for 20 more West Bank settlements in the next five years — a period coinciding with a transition period of Palestinian autonomy agreed upon by Egypt and Israel at the Camp David summit in September.

Israeli officials say Dayan's statement on settlement was in effect a reply to Egyptian Acting Foreign Minister Butros Ghali, who said the struggle for an independent Palestinian state will start after an Egyptian-Israeli peace treaty is signed.

The new settlements would show that Israel does not intend to be expelled from the West Bank, Dayan said.

Begin declared that an independent state controlled by the Palestinian Liberation Organization would be a danger not only to the security, but to the very existence of Israel.

January, 1979

1-7-79
Iran, Turkey violence said spurring Sadat.
Cairo, Egypt

President Anwar Sadat was quoted as saying that the situation in Turkey and Iran lends new urgency to signing a peace treaty with Israel and that he was ready to sign "right now."

Representative Donald Mitchell of New York declared Sadat is ready to sign the peace treaty today. What is happening in Turkey and Iran makes it vital "we act now."

Sadat was referring to the anti-Shah violence threatening the stability of Iran and to the bloody religious fighting in Turkey.

Sadat said Iran has disappeared as a buffer to Soviet influence in the Middle East and urged the congressmen, four of whom sit on the House Services Committee, to give Egypt new weapons to help defend the area.

Acting Egyptian Foreign Minister Butros Ghali said in Cairo that reports from Israeli diplomats that a meeting of low-level representatives would take place prior to another shuttle by Secretary of State Cyrus Vance were without basis.

Egypt and Israel have reassessed their positions since peace talks broke down last month and have declared their willingness to resume negotiations, but no new talks have been set.

The congressmen were to meet today with Israeli Prime Minister Menachem Begin in Israel.

1-14-79
New Mid-East plan
Washington, D.C.

The United States announced Saturday the start of a new, two-stage effort to conclude the negotiations for an Egyptian-Israeli peace treaty.
After weeks of consultations with Egypt and Israel on how best to resume the talks involving Secretary of State Cyrus Vance and senior Egyptian and Israeli officials in Washington. The Vance-level talks, which could include President Carter, will deal with key questions that have failed to be resolved after three months of sporadic negotiations. No date has been set for this set of negotiations.
Sadat, President of Egypt, has refused to sign the peace treaty, unless it was accompanied by guarantees that Israel would live up to its pledge to end military government and help establish the Palestinian councils on the West Bank and Gaza.

1-19-79
U.S. regrets new Israeli outposts.
Washington, D.C.

The United States has decided to register regret over Israel's decision to build three new settlements on land captured from the Arabs during the 1967 Mid-East war.
U.S. ambassador Samuel Lewis is under instruction in Jerusalem to advise the Israeli government that the Carter administration is concerned about the impact the decision could have on stalemated peace talks.
The expression of regret, disclosed by U.S. officials, is aimed at trying to persuade Israel not to go through with the three military outposts. Two are to be on the West Bank of the Jordan River and another in the Gaza district.
Meanwhile, Deputy Prime Minister Yigal Yadin told reporters that Israel must increase its military settlements in occupied territories for security reasons, apart from

reaching peace with Egypt.

On this, he said, there is "virtual unanimity" among the people of Israel, since it is unable to maintain troops on all exposed frontiers.

Jordan is only a few minutes flying time away, and Syria and Irag have recently moved toward a military union. "The Jordan valley is the exposed heart of Israel," Yadin replied. "Unless we protect the Jordan valley, we shall always be in danger."

1-22-79
The illusive peace

A lot of people around the world, and not least of all in the Middle East, are confused and disappointed that the peace agreement between Egypt and Israel, which seemed at hand after the Camp David breakthrough in September, has gone awry.

After agreeing on most substantive issues such as territorial boundaries, troop withdrawal schedules, and even the treaty test itself, Egypt and Israel seem to be prevented by political considerations from making minor concessions, largely symbolic, required for a full agreement.

The linkage between the Egyptian-Israeli settlement and autonomy for the Palestinians on the West Bank and Gaza Strip, a roadblock which the Camp David Accords sidestepped, appear to have become an impenetrable blockade as the result of external pressure on President Sadat and internal partisan pressures on Prime Minister Begin.

The treaty drafting process has been moving on schedule. The Israeli parliament and cabinet confirmed the Camp David understandings, including complete evacuation of the Sinai Peninsula, and Sadat announced plans for a treaty signing on Mount Sinai. The trouble began with an Arab summit meeting in Baghdad, Iraq, that was made significant by the unexpected attendance of Saudi Arabia, the chief financier of Egyptian economy.

Besides voting a $11 billion war chest aimed at Israel, the Arab conference mounted a blistering attack on Egypt's separate peace with Israel and threatened to expand the long-existent economic boycott against Israel to include Egypt as well.

Sadat began to change, insisting on specified linkage with the West Bank and making an exchange of ambassadors contingent upon a timetable of Israeli compliance. Sadat also proposed that Egypt's military commitments to its Arab allies take precedence over its treaty with Israel. Faced with a razor-thin parliamentary majority and rising criticism about further concessions, the Begin government flatly rejected these changes, despite pressure by the Carter administration.

The stalled, deadlocked negotiations are not back to square one as surface appearances might suggest. The distance covered by the Camp David Accords remain; the same basic interests of Egypt, Israel, and United States that will be served by a peace treaty are unchanged. The limits of possible concessions have been explored and defined. What remains is for the limits of compromise to be equally defined, the prerequisite for a cooling off period, a lowering of voices, and then a resumption of talks.

In the final analysis both parties should be motivated by the reality that failure will punish them, as it will proportionately reward the Soviet Union and most radical Arabs, including the Palestinian Liberation Organization.

1-29-79
Egypt seen as new Mid-East buffer
Cairo, Egypt

The impending arrival of a U.S. military delegation is seen as a new indication that the United States is counting on Egypt to replace Iran as a buffer to Soviet influence in the Middle East. A Pentagon delegation is due this week to expedite arms sales.

President Anwar Sadat, with visiting U.S. Congressmen, mentioned that Egypt needs more arms to assist pro-western regimes in Africa and the Persian Gulf. The situation in Iran threatens the entire Middle East. The turmoil may delay the signing of an Egyptian-Israeli peace treaty, or it may accelerate the agreements.

The Pentagon delegation is expected to visit Egypt and Saudi Arabia this week and will try to resolve financing the fighter plane (F-5) deliveries, approved by congress. Saudi Arabia agreed to purchase the package, believed to be over 700 million dollars, for Egypt, but the Saudi's have remained at odds with Sadat over his peacemaking with Israel.

The instability in Iran has provided a spur for all three countries to resolve the dispute in the name of a united front against Soviet influence.

February, 1979

2-5-79
Egypt declines summit meeting with Israel
Cairo, Egypt

Egypt has rejected an Israeli proposal for a summit meeting at the Sinai town of El Arish to resolve differences over a Mid-East peace settlement, a Cairo magazine, *Rose El Youssef,* reported.

The Israelis recommended that Prime Minister Menachem Begin and President Anwar Sadat meet in El Arish and called for President Carter's participation at a later stage.

Cairo's semi-official newspaper, *Al Ahram,* stated that President Carter of the United States is studying Ambassador's Alfred Atherton report and plans to contact Sadat after Red Chinese Vice Premier Teng Hsiao-Ping ends his visit to the United Stated today.

Egypt is continuing a cultural program with Israel that it started after last September's Camp David summit established a framework for peace.

The future of the Palestinians on the West Bank and in the Gaza Strip presents a problem and a stumbling block to a peace treaty between Israel and Egypt. Egypt insists that the treaty be linked to a timetable for implementing Palestinian home rule, while Israel fears failure to meet the timetable would endanger the treaty.

2-8-79
Egypt accepts talk invite
Cairo, Egypt

Egypt today accepted an American invitation to three-way ministerial level talks aimed at breaking the impasse in Mid-East talks with Israel.

The invitation was given to President Anwar Sadat by American Ambassador Hermann Eilts during a 40 minute meeting at the President's palace.

A similar invitation was given to Israeli Prime Minister Menachem Begin on February 6, 1979. The Israeli Cabinet met this morning to consider the invitation, but postponed the decision until its regular meeting the first of the week.

2-12-79
Israel accepts offer to meet with Egypt
Jerusalem

Israel accepted the American invitation to resume peace talks with Egypt at Camp David, Maryland, later this month but announced no softening of its stand on unresolved issues. Egypt accepted the invitation last week.

Prime minister Menachem Begin said there would be a break in the Camp David talks so Foreign Minister Moshe Dayan and Egyptian Prime Minister Mustafa Khalil could consult with their governments, an indication the talks may go beyond the three or four days originally planned.

Begin said the Cabinet took no new policy decisions that would release Dayan from earlier positions in his talks with Khalil and Secretary of State Cyrus Vance.

The Camp David meeting is likely to focus on how an Egyptian-Israeli peace treaty should relate to the Palestinian issue and how to ensure neither side can retreat from its commitments if difficulties arise in subsequent talks over the West Bank of Jordan and the Gaza Strip.

Egypt is demanding a target date for the beginning of Palestinian self-government in the areas now ruled by an Israeli military government. But Israel says it cannot agree since there is no guarantee the Palestinians will cooperate.

In addition, Egypt opposes an Israeli demand that a treaty supersede any previous Egyptian defense treaties.

At the Camp David summit last September, Begin and President Anwar Sadat agreed on a basic outline for autonomy for the one million Palestinians in the West Bank and Gaza, but left the details for negotiations that are to start one month after a bilateral treaty is signed.

A Cabinet-appointed committee submitted a 300-page document recommending that Israel adopt a tough approach to the autonomy agreement and limit the authority of a proposed Palestinian governing council.

The report recommends that self-rule apply only to the West Bank and Gaza Arabs, and not to the land itself. That means Israel would remain in charge of state owned land, water resources, and approximately 5000 Israeli citizens in Jewish settlements.

Joint Israeli Palestinian committees would oversee water allocations and propose legislation. The self-governing authority could levi taxes, but could not issue money or passports, according to the recommendations.

2-19-79
Israel's General Sharon
Washington, D.C.

While Iran severs its Western ties for a Moslem-style republic, one of Israel's more charismatic leaders is talking tougher than ever about his countries' long range plans to bring Palestinian West Bank under permanent Israeli control.

General Ariel Sharon, who was put in charge of the Jewish settlements issue by Prime Minister Menachem

Begin, is publicly plotting a future for more than one million West Bank Palestinians— most of them Moslems — that could drastically lengthen the odds against success of President Carter's newest Jerusalem-Cairo mediation effort.

The effort starts next week when Israeli and Egyptian foreign ministers meet in a renewal of Camp David, but under conditions pessimistic compared to the outcome of the Camp David summit last fall.

What disturbs top officials is that Sharon risks stirring up dormant religious passions on the West Bank and in East Jerusalem, one of Islam's holiest places, at a time when Moslem fundamentalists showed sufficient strength to fire up the Iranian revolution and now threatens sectarian reactions elsewhere.

"Sharon is Begin's Andy Young," one well-placed authority said, He speaks with the Ambassador's conviction about the way things ought to be, but in his heart he knows that it is not possible."

Sharon was a true hero in the October, 1973, Israeli-Egyptian war, and is convinced that expansion of the Jewish settlements on the Arab-populated West Bank will ensure better protection in planning of roads and highways and territorial continuity between (new) cities and older settlements.

The land for this Israeli takeover of large portions of the West Bank must be seized "without delay." Asked if the seizure of lands might not weaken the changes of Egypt signing a peace treaty agreement with Israel, and of Jordan and the Palestinians negotiating self-rule, Sharon said it would not.

"Seizure of lands does not increase friction with the Arab population. It will prevent such friction in the future."

The view of Arab reactions to the loss of their historic lands reminded some authorities here of Andrew Young, Ambassador of the United States. He regarded Fidel Castro's Cuban troops in Angola as a stabilizing force of the African Countries. Neither view is in accord with political facts.

It is doubtful that Sharon will be able to impress the Begin government with his large scale development for the West Bank. If he were wrong in his appraisals, the religious fanatics in Iran could spread to Moslem Jerusalem and the West Bank, introducing a lethal element that would destroy Israel.

2-21-79
New Israeli-Egyptian talks open Camp David secrecy
Washington, D.C.

Egyptian and Israeli negotiators, meeting in the sumptuous seclusion of Camp David, opened a new round of talks today to see if a long-elusive peace treaty can be concluded under U.S. auspices.

Secretary of State Cyrus Vance boarded a helicopter at the snow-banked Pentagon in the early morning and flew to the presidential retreat for breakfast at Maple Lodge with Egyptian Prime Minister Mustafa Khalil and Israeli Foreign Minister Moshe Dayan.

U.S. officials confirmed that Egyptian President Anwar Sadat had requested a broad range of modern American weaponry, while offering to play a major pro-Western military role in the Middle East.

President Carter of the United States may join the conference at Camp David, and include Prime Minister Menachem Begin and President Sadat if an accord can be reached.

The principal stumbling block in the path of an agreement is the Palestinian issue. Israel has offered civil autonomy to the one million Palestinian Arabs on the West Bank of the Jordan River and in the Gaza district, but Egypt wants the details including a treaty package rather than subsequent neogtiations.

On the eve of the talks, the government-controlled radio in Cairo, Egypt sounded a cry by saying, "there is no place left for maneuvering and procrastination."

Meanwhile, Israeli sources stated that Foreign Minister Moshe Dayan would stress a need for the United States in financing new air fields in the Negev Desert to replace the ones in the Sinai that will be turned over to Egypt.

With Iran ending its Israeli oil shipments, there will be stress on arrangements for Israel to share in the production of the Sinai offshore oil fields.

Developed by Israel with the help of U.S. firms, they now provide about 15 per cent of Israel's needs.

2-22-79
Egypt-Israel peace talks need push from the U.S.

The negotiations between Israel and Egypt that reopened on February 21, 1979 at Camp David may produce an accord if both sides can demonstrate flexibility, and if the United States can offer concrete and helpful proposals, and can give the Israeli and Egyptian foreign ministers something foundational for a peace settlement.

There are three items in dispute. All provide room for maneuvering and procrastination, because of unrest in Iran, that makes Israel fearful, and the Arab world belligerent.

One disputed point might go either way without serious effect. The draft treaty provides that the Sinai securities agreement "may at the request of either party be reviewed and amended by mutual agreement of the parties." Egypt wants to change "may" to "shall." The practical effect would be minimal. Israel would have to assent to a review, but it would not have to agree to an amendment. Israel's objection is that the change would suggest that the security arrangements aren't permanent. Egypt says that any suggestion of permanence is an affront to Egyptian sovereignty.

Another item in dispute is the requirement that Egypt regard its obligations under the treaty as superior to those of its 1951 mutual security agreement with other Arab nations. Egypt states that Israel does not need that strong a provision, because no Arab country would attack Israel without Egypt's help. Then why shouldn't it say its treaty with Israel comes first?

The third disputed point in the negotiations is the one most important to Egyptian President Anwar Sadat. Sadat insists on a link between normalization of Egyptian-Isaeli relations and elections for Palestinians living in the West Bank of the Jordan River and in the Gaza Strip. Under Sadat's proposal, which has been rejected by the Israeli cabinet, ambassadors would be exchanged when the elections were held. The end of 1979 would be set as the target date.

Sadat has room to give on the first two points, if he can do so without appearing to other Arab leaders to be surrendering too much to Israel.

Israel can bend on Palestinian elections, if it decides it can rely on United States' guarantees that Egypt will not be allowed to violate other treaty positions.

The key to success in these talks will be the U.S. stance and the U.S. proposals.

2-26-79
New round of Mid-East talks urged.
Washington, D.C.

President Carter, determined to "spare no effort" for peace in the Middle East, called for a new Camp David summit conference to try to conclude a treaty between Israel and Egypt.

The talks would be held, beginning later in the week, with Prime Minister Menachem Begin representing Israel, but without participation of Egyptian President Anwar Sadat.

Egypt would be represented by Prime Minister Mustafa Khalil, who had been authorized by Sadat to conclude the negotiations. There was no official explanation for Sadat's absence.

Carter made the announcement at the windup of four days of treaty negotiations between Khalil and Israeli Foreign Minister Moshe Dayan.

Secretary of State Cyrus Vance is known to have presented new U.S. proposals on the Palestinian issue during his discussions with Dayan and Khalil.

President Carter said before the talks began that he might convene a summit if the ministerial negotiations indicated the two countries were determined to complete the treaty.

In Cairo, meanwhile, the Middle East news agency reported that Khalil would fly directly home instead of stopping in London, England, as initially planned.

2-27-79
Israel to decide Begin's role in the peace talks.
Jerusalem

Israel's Cabinet is meeting to decide whether Prime Menachem Begin will accept a U.S. invitation to a Mid-East conference meeting without Egyptian President Anwar Sadat.

Foreign Minister Moshe Dayan flew in from Washington to attend the crucial session.

Some Israeli leaders have voiced doubts that Sadat's representative, Mustafa Khalil, would have the power to make decisions at a summit and said they feared the meeting could lead to pressuring Israel alone on issues blocking a peace treaty.

Sadat, meanwhile, kept silent on why he sent Khalil to Camp David rather than personally attending.

One of the President's aides stated that Sadat should not be expected to "do everything" and it was fitting for Khalil to represent Egypt since both he and Begin are Prime Ministers.

When President Carter announced his plans for a summit, he left Sadat the option of joining the talks if they proved successful.

The Egyptian newspaper Al Ahram has stated Egypt's views regarding the proposed agreement, that Khalil has submitted a written memorandum to Dayan and Secretary of State Cyrus Vance requesting the adoption of five "urgent steps concerning Jewish settlements, public freedom, measures undertaken by the Israeli occupation authority, and the necessity of reducing Israeli military forces in the cities of the West Bank and the Gaza Strip."

2-28-79
Israel rejects the new peace proposals
Tel Aviv, Israel

Israel's rejection of an American invitation to Prime Minister Menachem Begin to attend an Israeli-Egyptian summit was a black day in the calendar of Mid-East peace talks.

When Egyptian President Anwar Sadat took the first step by visiting Jerusalem 15 months ago, he and Begin said they could reach a peace treaty in two or three months.

Last September, the two leaders and President Carter produced the Camp David accords and vowed to sign a treaty within three months. The handshakes and embraces Sadat and Begin exchanged at the White House were their last contact.

SUMMARY: This is a recap of the major events in the search for Mid-East peace:

Nov. 19, 1977
Israel is bedecked with Egyptian flags for Sadat's 44-hour visit. While offering to negotiate security for Israel, Sadat calls for a complete Israeli withdrawal from Arab lands captured in 1967 and for Palestinian national rights.

Dec. 25, 1977
Begin travels to Ismalia, Egypt, for a summit with Sadat and presents Israel's plan for a withdrawal from the Sinai Peninsula and limited self-rule for Palestinians living in the West Bank of the Jordan River and the Gaza Strip.

Jan. 17-18, 1978
The Jerusalem foreign ministers conference breaks down suddenly as Sadat calls his delegation home, the first indication of major difficulty in reaching an agreement.

Jan. - Sept., 1978
Israeli Defense Minister Ezer Weizman strikes a rapport with Sadat. Secretary of State Cyrus Vance and his troubleshooter for the Mid-East, Alfred Atherton, travel the region again and again. Vice-President Walter Mondale makes the Mid-East shuttle in June, and a foreign ministers conference is held at Leeds Castle, England in July. Israel agrees to negotiate the final status of the West Bank and Gaza after a five-year period of self-rule.

Sept. 6-17, 1978
Carter, risking a monumental failure, coaches Sadat and Begin through the Camp David summit resulting in two accords, one outlining an Israel-Egyptian treaty, the other a framework for Palestinian self-rule in the West Bank and Gaza.

Oct. 11 - Nov. 12, 1978
Israeli and Egyptian ministers meet in the Blair House, Washington D.C., to finish drafting the Israel-Egypt treaty. Israel charges that Egypt was trying to alter the Camp David accords by linking the treaty to implementation of Palestinian self-rule. This linkage is a must for Egypt's effort to avoid the appearance of signing a separate peace with Israel. Israel rejects an American proposal setting the end of 1979 as a target date for Palestinian autonomy.

Dec. 17, 1978
The three months deadline for signing a treaty passes. Vance meets Israeli Foreign Minister Moshe Dayan and Egyptian Prime Minister Mustafa Khalil in Brussels, laying ground work for their conference in Washington in February.

Feb. 25, 1979
Carter summons Dayan and Khalil to the White House and tells reporters he will invite Begin to a summit with Khalil and Carter himself at Camp David. Sadat will not attend.

Feb. 27, 1979
Though Dayan helped draft Carter's statement, Begin's Cabinet rejects it, saying Egypt is taking "a more extreme position." Begin claims, "The peace process will continue."

March, 1979

3-1-79
Key Egyptian demands backed by the U.S.
Washington D.C.

The United States, in its drive to break the deadlock in Mid-East peace treaty negotiations, is supporting key Egyptian demands in the dispute with Israel, diplomatic sources said today.

Specifically, the Carter administration agrees with Egypt that a one-year timetable be set for establishing Palestinian civil autonomy in Israeli-held territories.

Under the U.S. proposals, Egyptian President Anwar Sadat and Israeli Prime Minister Menachem Begin would agree to a timetable in exchange of letters that would be part of the treaty package.

The Carter administration also supports the Egyptian position that the treaty with Israel should not have priority over Egypt's military ties with other Arab countries.

The U.S. formula, presented to the two sides by Secretary of State Cyrus Vance last week at Camp David under tight secrecy, provides that Egypt and Israel reserve their ability to act in collective self-defense.

Treaty terms agreed to last fall by Egyptian and Israeli negotiators gave peace between the two countries precedence over the Arab defense pacts. Sadat later requested that the terms be revised. He also has insisted on a timetable for Palestinian autonomy.

Israel objects to both demands.

Prime Minister Menachem Begin arrives this evening for critical talks with President Carter. He has received secret instructions from his cabinet that criticizes the

United States for supporting Egyptian proposals unacceptable to Israel.

On a third key point, President Carter is supporting Sadat in withholding an exchange of ambassadors with Israel until all of Sinai is returned to Egypt and steps are taken toward Palestinian autonomy.

The two countries would establish embassies on each other's land and exchange lower-level diplomats.

3-1-79
Israel — Egypt peace treaty in crisis situation.

Problems of the Camp David peace treaty may be magnified if the Camp David Accords leave Israel vulnerable to harassment from Arab reactionaries.

President Carter's public insistence that the differences between Egypt and Israel are insignificant adds to the pressure on Prime Minister Menachem Begin, since Egyptian President Anwar Sadat has said he will not budge from his demands. The pressure was increased by the President of the United States saying he would be "frank" in the discussions, and was further heightened by the President's announcement that after he met with Begin he expected to invite Khalil, Prime Minister of Egypt, or possibly Sadat to join in the talks.

The President's negotiations were adequate in their first test, but time and the events in Iran have made the second test far more difficult. The world can only pray that careful diplomacy and President Carter's ability to negotiate solutions are equal to the demands of the current crisis.

3-4-79
Begin balks in Mid-East treaty talks.
Washington D.C.

The U.S. peace drive appears to be running out of steam as Israeli Prime Minister Menachem Begin gives no sign of yielding to Egyptian demands that have the support of President Carter.

Secretary of State Cyrus Vance and other key advisers have prepared for Carter a number of undisclosed and highly tentative ideas that they hope might break the impasse.

U. S. officials declined to divulge any of the details and seemed gloomy about the course of the negotiations. However, one approach was understood to involve possible U.S. security measures to protect Israel if Begin yields on key remaining issues.

In striving to break the impasse, President Carter is focusing his energies on trying to gain compromises from Begin. There is no parallel effort at this point with Egypt.

The Israeli leader vowed on his arrival of March 1, 1979, that he could not be pressed into signing "a sham document." He warned that the negotiations were in deep crisis.

The major unresolved issues include:

Whether a timetable for establishing Palestinian autonomy in Israeli held territory will be attached to the treaty.

Whether the treaty should take priority over Egypt's military ties with other Arab countries.

Sadat's refusal to exchange ambassadors with Israel, until all of the Sinai territory held by Israel is relinquished.

3-5-79
Carter proposes conclusive plans.
Washington D.C.

President Carter, in a fresh effort to salvage Mid-East peace prospects gave Israeli Prime Minister Menachem Begin new proposals described by an Israeli official as "important and interesting."

The contents were kept secret, but Senator Jacob Javits, Republican of New York state, told reporters after a congressional meeting with the president that the proposals were in the nature of "pragmatic guarantees" designed to build trust between Egypt and Israel.

"It may be the cement that binds this treaty," Javits stated. He refused to provide further details.

Begin referred the proposals to his government in Jerusalem and told President Carter he hoped to have a response before he leaves the United States.

Meanwhile, a White House statement said Carter would review the situation with Egyptian President Anwar Sadat. Senator Percy, Republican of Illinois, said the two leaders were already in touch.

"I think he's gone the last mile," Percy replied of the President's intensive effort to guide Egypt and Israel to completion of the illusive treaty.

Egypt's President Anwar Sadat, getting regular reports on the Carter-Begin talks in Washington, says he will have "lots" to tell the world today about Cairo's next step in the push for a Mid-East peace.

Sadat received a progress report on the talks yesterday from Ambassador Hermann Eilts. He said he would be discussing the reports with his vice-president, Hosny Mubarak and Prime Minister Mustafa Khalil.

3-5-79
President Carter departs for the Mid-East on Wednesday March 7, 1979
Washington D.C.

President Carter will fly to the Middle East Wednesday in an effort to salvage hope for peace between Israel and Egypt, the White House announced today.

White House press secretary Jody Powell said Carter will arrive in Egypt on Thursday afternoon for talks with President Anwar Sadat and will proceed to Israel on Saturday for discussions with Prime Minister Menachem Begin.

Begin, speaking to a group of congressmen, and Egyptian Prime Minister Mustafa Khalil, in a telephone interview with The Associated Press in Cairo, both expressed hope that Carter's journey would result in the signing of a peace treaty.

"Let us hope Egypt will join this effort," Begin said.

"Then, if this happens, in a short period of time we may have the ceremony of signing."

"I do not think that an American president, when he decides to visit Egypt and Israel, would leave the Accords to fate.

The announcement of the trip came about two hours after Begin told Carter at a surprise White House meeting that the Israeli cabinet has responded positively to U.S. suggestions for resolving some of the remaining obstacles to an Israeli- Egyptian peace treaty.

The President's travel plans will focus on the peace process, regional security and bilateral issues.

"The President believes that we must not allow the prospects for peace, which seemed so bright last September to continue to dim and perhaps to vanish. If we do, the Judgment of history and of our children will rightly condemm us."

3-6-79
Carter resolves to complete Mid-East peace treaty
Washington D.C.

After a series of meetings between President Carter and Prime Minister Menachem Begin, beginning last Thursday, the U.s. mediation effort appeared to be headed toward defeat, but late Sunday March 4, 1979, after four sessions, there was a sudden reversal.

The President of the United States gave Begin new U.S. proposals for breaking the deadlock. They were submitted to the Israeli cabinet, which voted Monday to accept them. The Prime Minister reported the action to Carter at a ten-minute White House meeting. The press secretary announced that President Carter will fly to Egypt and Israel beginning Wednesday of this week.

The Israeli cabinet vote of 9-3 with four abstensions was a sign of considerable opposition within the cabinet, indicating Israel made some hard concessions in accepting the proposals.

The principal sticking point has been President Sadat's

demand, backed by the Carter administration, that a timetable be included in the treaty package for establishing self-rule on the West Bank of the Jordan River and in Gaza. An informed source in Jerusalem said Israel made some movement on that demand.

Another problem which the U.S. proposals also reportedly dealt with was the clause saying the treaty supersedes all previous conflicting agreements. Sadat, backed by the United States, has insisted that the treaty not take precedence over Egypt's commitment to assist other Arab countries in wars of self-defense against Israel.

Begin met with more than 50 U.S. senators for over an hour Monday afternoon and told reporters later he believes Sadat can accept the new proposals.

Several senators who were in the meeting said they gained the impression one major U.S. proposal deals with assurances to Israel that Egypt would live up to peace treaty terms despite what other arrangements it might have with Arab governments.

3-7-79
Israel accepts three Carter proposals
Jerusalem

Israel agrees to three compromises proposed by President Carter that may break through the barriers preventing an Egyptian-Israeli peace treaty.

In New York, Prime Minister Menachem Begin was asked to compare his feelings now and at the time of last year's Camp David summit meeting. He replied: "There was euphoria, not only in this country, but in Cairo and Jerusalem and throughout the world. Now we must be very careful. I am hopeful."

In Cairo, President Anwar Sadat met with U.S. National Security Adviser Zbigniew Brzezinski to hear the details of Carter's proposals. Sadat's reaction was not immediately known, but Egyptian officials said the President of United State's trip to the Middle East may mean "the final sprint" to a peace treaty.

Sources with firsthand knowledge of the proposals, which have not been revealed, said they involved two compromises on linking the treaty to the Palestinian problem and the third on softening language about whether the treaty would supersede prior defense agreements.

These two issues have been the crux of the disagreement since Egyptian and Israeli delegations formulated a draft treaty in Washington last November. Neither Jerusalem nor Cairo was satisfied with the draft.

Without disclosing the precise language of all the U.S. proposals, the sources, who declined to be identified, outlined them as follows:

Israel agrees to a 12-month non-binding target date for completing negotiations on self-rule for the one million Palestinians living on the occupied West Bank and the Gaza Strip.

There is, however, no deadline for establishing autonomy, but Israel pledges to carry out the plan as quickly as possible. There is a safeguard Israel has demanded in the event the Palestinians reject the plan.

In a second point linking the treaty to the Palestinian problem, Israel agrees to language specifying that the treaty does not contradict the Camp David framework for a general Mid-East peace.

A clause remains unchanged in the draft saying the treaty will be carried out, "without regard to action or inaction by any other party and independently of any instrument external to this treaty."

Again, this adds to the linkage so important to Sadat without setting deadlines or penalties for non-compliance. The Egyptian leader has been condemned by other Arab states for his unilateral peace move, so he has pressed for some connection in the treaty solving the Palestinian problem.

The third modification has to do with the language in the treaty's "priority clause," which has been altered to satisfy Egypt's objections that the treaty appears to invalidate its earlier defense pacts with Arab states. The proposed compromise softens the wording so both sides can feel their interests are protected.

3-8-79
Mid-East peace treaty within reach.
Washington D.C.

Declaring that peace in the Mid-East has come within reach, President Carter departs today for treaty negotiations in Cairo and Jerusalem.

Carter said his hope for a treaty is "tempered by sober realism." He reminded the Israelis he expects them eventually to conclude a broader comprehensive peace settlement that would resolve the touchy Palestinian question.

Egyptian officials are calling Carter's mission the final lap to peace, but many details remain to completely wrap up a treaty between Egypt and Israel.

The President of the United States, speaking on the south lawn of the White House before departing, said real peace in the Middle East will not come until Israel strikes a comprehensive peace agreement with all her Arab neighbors, not just Egypt. The treaty between Israel and Egypt is an indispensable step toward a broader understanding of peace we all seek in the Middle East and Asia.

3-8-79
Compromise or confrontation
Washington D.C.

On the two major and highly complicated foreign policy problems now facing the United States — the control of strategic arms and accomodation between Israel and Egypt — President Carter is asking a simple human question.

Would the world be better off with an inadequate compromise agreement on both issues or with no agreement at all?

Carter obviously believes that even a quarter loaf is better than no bread. He is not saying that a SALT treaty on the terms now available will control the arms race, or that the Camp David Accords, as amended at the White House recently, will bring peace to the Middle East.

These compromises are better than nothing, and will keep the peace process going.

The President of the United States argues there must be restraints on the development of new military weapons systems, and in the Middle East an effort will be made to persuade Sadat and Begin to settle, at least temporarily, the differences that exist between Egypt and Israel, and to promote friendship and understanding for a lasting peace with all the Arab nations.

Since Prime Minister Begin took office in Jerusalem the Communists have taken control of Angola, Yemen, Ethopia, Afghanistan, and at the present time are creating revolution in Iran. In order to safeguard the interests of the United States and its allies, a defense must be established to prevent the Reds from extending any further, imperiling the rest of the world's balance of power.

President Carter arrives in Egypt
Cairo, Egypt

President Carter arrives in Egypt to the tens of thousands of cheering Egyptians and confers with President Anwar Sadat for over two hours on the alterations of the peace treaty with Israel. A U.S. official said Egypt's leaders were "not too happy" with American compromise terms.

Egypt presented its own counter-proposal, but the changes were not disclosed. The two leaders discussed unresolved issues in a quest for an Israeli-Egyptian peace accord, but a breakthrough was not negotiated.

Both Khalil and Israeli Prime Minister Menachem Begin have said that Carter's trip could lead to a treaty signing.

Sadat has insisted on a timetable for civil autonomy for Palestinians that Begin has promised. Begin, in turn, has opposed linking the Palestinian problem to the treaty. A reported compromise would set a target date for implementing autonomy, but no hard deadline.

Khalil said the U.S. proposals were "negotiable and can be modified according to our ideas." His comments were the first indication that suggestions were not entirely satisfactory to the Egyptians.

Carter will remain in Egypt until Saturday night, when he flies to Israel for consultations with Begin. There is a possibility that if an agreement is solidified, Secretary of State Cyrus Vance will remain in the region to complete the details.

3-9-79
Carter visits Alexandria, Egypt
Alexandria, Egypt

Rolling through the Nile Delta on a slow train, President Carter and Egypt's Anwar Sadat said today problems and misunderstandings still block an Egyptian-Israeli treaty.

Plans were being made for Secretary of State Cyrus Vance to explain the treaty to leaders in Jordan and Saudi Arabia, if the agreement is concluded, or to work on remaining details, if there is no pact.

The Egyptian leader said he is ready to sign a treaty, but Israeli misunderstanding and mistrust block the way. He said that only some "words" now separate the two nations.

In Israel, Prime Minister Menachem Begin spent three hours briefing his cabinet and said afterward, "Everything now depends on the Egyptian answer; Israel has done its part."

"I'm doing my best," Sadat stated today, "but without the intensive effort by President Carter and the American people, we would have never reached a position in which a treaty is within reach."

3-11-79
Mid-East peace with Begin and Sadat near
Jerusalem

President Carter, strongly hinting that a peace accord is near, carried Egypt's proposals to crucial talks with Israeli

Prime Minister Menachem Begin. The two leaders held "frank" discussions for an hour and a half on some minor changes of the peace treaty.

The President of the United States made an optimistic statement on his arrival in Tel Aviv. "I have good reason to hope that the goal can now be reached for a permanent and lasting peace with Israel and Egypt."

On the second leg of his peace journey that began in Egypt, Carter said, "It would be a tragedy to turn away from the path of peace after having come so far."

Arriving at the end of the Jewish Sabbath, the President and his wife, Rosalyn, were greeted by Begin and President Yitzak Navon.

Navon declared that Israel had made "enormous sacrifices far beyond what was expected" to achieve peace.

Carter stated, "It is in the nature of negotiations that no treaty can be ideal from either the Egyptian or Israeli point of view. My friends, my brothers, let us complete the work before us. Let us find peace together."

3-12-79
Peace in Mid-East angers Arab Coalition
Beirut, Lebanon

Why are so many Arabs angry about the prospect of peace between Egypt and Israel?

At first glance, the heavy flow of criticism from Arab capitals toward President Carter's current peace mission suggests that the majority of Arabs prefer a state of war, and will not be satisfied until Israel disappears.

This conclusion does not seem accurate from the views of the vast majority of Arabian common people. The feeling on the streets, and in government interior departments, appears to be that peace is preferable to the status of the past three decades, and Israel is here to stay, for better or for worse.

The proposed treaty does little to satisfy the Palestinian problem, which in recent years has become the prime irritant in the Arab-Israeli conflict. The plan for Palestinian autonomy on the West Bank of the Jordan River and the Gaza Strip involves the one million current residents, but ignores more than three million other Palestinians who live in refugee camps and elsewhere as the result of the establishment of Israel in 1948. The plan also denies the Palestinians an independent state, to which Arab regimes have pledged themselves, and leaves Israel in fundamental control of the occupied regions.

The plan keeps Israel in control of the Arab sector of Jerusalem, which contains Islam's third holiest shrine, and of Syria's Golan Heights. Both areas were wrested from Arab control in the 1967 Mideast War.

A separate Egyptian peace deprives the Arab world of its largest army, Egypt's, thus weakening the overall Arab bargaining position for extracting concessions from Israel.

This is the main reason other Arab leaders have spurned President Anwar Sadat's call to join him in making peace with Israel. Convinced that Sadat has only his and Egypt's interests at heart, they believe they would be dealing with their traditional enemy primarily on Israel's terms and against their interests.

The potential loss of Egypt, which has traditionally been the seat of Islamic culture, from the Arab fold has deep psychological effects as well.

After the loss of the southern front against Israel, radical Arabs are likely to fear that the moderates would give up and join the peace process. Some diplomatic observers believe that is one reason Iraq is cementing ties with its old nemesis, Syria, to help keep the Syrians from slipping toward the American camp on the heels of Egypt.

The same fear applies to Jordan, where King Hussein is managing to keep militant nerves quiet by taking a hard line against the Camp David Accord worked out last September by Carter, Sadat, and Prime Minister Menachem Begin of Israel.

3-12-79
President Carter delays his departure
Jerusalem

President Carter delayed his departure from Israel today. It is reported he will not leave for Cairo, Egypt until tomorrow, after making what Prime Minister Menachem Begin called "great progress" in his quest for an Egyptian-Israeli peace treaty.

After hearing the results of an all-night Israeli cabinet meeting, the U.S. President told members of the Parliament that leaders of Israel and Egypt are not ready to risk a peace treaty, "although, their people are ready now," for peace.

At the Knesset, Carter opened his remarks by saying that in the preceding 24 hours he had discarded two draft speeches, one "a speech on despair" and the other "a speech of glad tidings and celebration."

"I have decided to deliver a speech of concern and caution," replied the President. It is now the responsibility of all parties "to contemplate the tragedy of failure, and legitimate exultation if we bring peace. . . Our vision must be as great as our goals. Wisdom and courage are required of us all."

He held out a promise of increased U.S. aid for Israel once a treaty is signed, pledging "new and stronger and more meaningful dimensions" to U.S. - Israeli relations.

"This is a very delicate stage of the negotiations," The Prime Minister stated. "I am hopeful, always We carefully examined all the conditions presented to us by the American delegation and agreed, some by majority vote and others by concensus to accept the alterations."

3-13-79
Peace breakthrough in Mid-East

President Carter ended his six-day Mid-East peace mission today, claiming a breakthrough for peace, but still short of the treaty he sought between Egypt and Israel.

Israeli Prime Minister Menachem Begin immediately said a treaty could be signed this month, possibly within the next week or two, if his cabinet and the Knesset approve a draft accord.

Staking his political career on compromises proposed by Carter, the Israeli leader stated that if the Knesset did not approve them, it would be the duty of his government, "to resign."

Carter said Egypt's President Anwar Sadat today accepted U.S. compromise proposals "for resolving the few remaining issues," and that Begin agreed to submit these compromises to his cabinet at the earliest opportunity.

In an Israeli radio interview broadcast nationwide, Begin said, "Just think what a turning point this will be, if we have peace with Egypt."

The President of the United States did not specify the shape of the compromise proposals, but they were believed to be Israel's desire for Sinai oil, Egypt's desire for liason officials to supervise Palestinian self-rule in Gaza, and Israel's desire for a quick exchange of ambassadors.

"I am convinced that we now have defined all the main ingredients of a peace treaty between Egypt and Israel which will be a cornerstone of a comprehensive peace settlement for the Middle East," Carter said at a Cairo airport, before his departure to the United States. "It is now up to Israel and Egypt."

3-14-79
Begin and Sadat approve treaty issues.

Shortly after the Israeli cabinet overwhelmingly approved the American-sponsored proposals in Jerusalem, President Carter issued a statement saying Prime Minister Menachem Begin "has just called me with good news."

He congratulated Begin and Egyptian President Anwar Sadat and added:

"The peace which their peoples so clearly need and want is close to reality."

"I am extremely pleased that the Israeli Cabinet has approved the proposals that I discussed with Prime Minister Begin in Jerusalem," Carter said in a brief statement.

"This means that all of the outstanding issues in the

negotiations between Egypt and Israel have now been successfully resolved."

The President said he is proud that the United States could have been able to assist the two Mid-East nations toward a peace treaty. "We stand ready to help in the implementation of the peace treaty, in the negotiations that lie ahead on other issues of concern, and in working with these two friends to build a stable and peaceful Middle East."

The Israeli cabinet vote was 15 in favor with one abstention after nearly six hours of debate. The cabinet, which met in emergency session in Jerusalem at Begin's request, was expected to send the treaty proposals to Israel's parliament, the Knesset. The Knesset was expected to approve the treaty.

Begin said he, Sadat, and Carter would sign the accord in Washington. Then, he and Sadat would sign the Hebrew version in Jerusalem and the Arabic text in Cairo.

3-16-79
Sadat must placate Arab leaders.

Egyptian President Anwar Sadat has dealt successfully with the Israelis, and now he must deal with his fellow Arabs.

Across much of the Arab world the official and unexpected response to Sadat's agreement to an Egyptian-Israeli peace treaty has been expressed in terms of shock, outrage, and condemnation. The personal slanders Sadat has heard and dismissed before. Reprisals may be more directed to Egypt.

There is no shortage of proposed threats and sanctions. Some of the more radical want to drum Egypt out of the Arab League, and move the organization's headquarters from Cairo. The Palestinian Liberation Organization has hinted at terrorist acts. The most substantive and damaging possibility is that Saudi Arabia, Kuwait, and other donors of cash may cut or end the subsidies they have been providing Egypt.

Sadat has weighed all of these punitive possibilities, and clearly has concluded that they count for less than the benefits he expects from formally ending his conflict with Israel. He does not welcome the political and psychological isolation that other Arabs threaten to impose on him, but neither does he seem to fear it. Long before his courageous initiative to Jerusalem in November, 1977, Sadat emphasized that Egypt's interests must take primacy.

Sadat has agreed to an honorable peace with Israel. With it he will restore to Egypt all of the Sinai Peninsula, vitally reclaiming the dignity lost by past military defeats. And he will get for the Palestinians, in the Gaza Strip, a greater measure of political autonomy than Palestinians ever had before, whether under the Turks, the British, the Jordanians, the Israelis, or the Egyptians.

Sadat says: Test comes after the signing of the accord
Cairo, Egypt

Anwar Sadat warned Israel that the "real test" of the Mid-East peace will come after their treaty is signed, when he and Prime Minister Begin will debate over the Palestinian self-rule.

A faction of the Israeli Cabinet, meanwhile, demanded a tougher stand on the Palestinian issue.

In Lebanon, Palestine Liberation Organization chief Yassar Arafat declared that Palestinian resistance in the West Bank of the Jordan River is a "time bomb" that will wreck the U.S. - Egyptian "plot."

Syrian radio broadcasts said Arafat would go to Amman, Jordan to confer with King Hussein, the moderate monarch who has refused to back the Israeli-Egyptian peace plans. Arafat's trip will put him ahead of a U.S. delegation also planning to meet with Hussein and seek his support. The visit by Arafat will be his first to Amman since Palestinian guerillas were ousted from Jordan in bloody fighting in 1970.

A high level U.S. delegation, including Adviser Zbigniew Brezinski and President Carter's son Chip, was heading for the Middle East and meetings with the leaders of Saudi Arabia and Jordan, two Arab states whose support for the treaty is crucial to the success of the U.S.-sponsored peace campaign.

Egyptian Vice-President Hosny Mubarak met with French President Valery Giscard d'Estaing in Paris to try to enlist his support. He had conferred with Saudi King Khaled, and press reports said he failed to win the King's backing.

In Cairo, Foreign Minister Butros Ghali met with Arab envoys from Saudi Arabia, Tunisia, The United Arab Emirates, Qatar, Mauritania, Morocco, Samalia, Oman and Bahrain to explain the treaty terms.

President Sadat, speaking with reporters during a visit to his home village in Northern Egypt said, "The real test of the peace process starts after the signing (of the treaty) — it is not the signing itself."

3-19-79
Arabs portray Mid-East treaty as triumph
Cairo, Egypt

A Cairo newspaper published the first full text of the Egyptian-Israeli peace treaty, and the government controlled media considered the pact as a triumph for all Arabs, although it contained no direct solution to the sticky Palestinian issue.

As published in the *Al-Ahram,* the body of the treaty is virtually identical to the accords published by the State Department last November, this despite bitter haggling and new demands made by both sides in the intervening months.

Egyptian Prime Minister Mustafa Khalil told the 312-member parliament organization of the ruling Democratic Party that the treaty gives Egypt and the Palestinians all they demanded.

Al Ahram also printed the interpretive documents attached to the treaty and a letter to be exchanged between Egypt and Israel.

The interpretive documents and the letter, which apparently made the treaty acceptable to both sides, were mostly the work of President Carter on his mediation mission to the Middle East last week.

Khalil claims the final form ensures linkage between the Egypt-Israel treaty, which essentially deals with Israeli withdrawal from the Sinai Peninsula, and action to set up Palestinian self-rule in the West Bank of the Jordan River and the Gaza Strip. "We have ensured Palestinian rights, regained our lands, and set the stage for other Arab powers to join in the peace process and resolve the Middle East problem decisively."

The treaty provides for Israeli withdrawal from 75 percent of the Sinai in nine months, with the remainder of the peninsula to be vacated in three years after ratification documents are exchanged.

The treaty also accords Israel free navigation in the Suez Canal and the Tiran Strait. The two countries are to have normal relations, including an exchange of ambassadors, as well as trade and cultural ties.

3-20-79
Egypt, Israel, dispute over Palestine

Israel and Egypt clashed today over the future of Jerusalem and the Palestinians in their first public disagreement since President Carter's visit to iron out final obstacles to a peace treaty.

Prime Minister Menachem Begin told Parliament in Jerusalem that Israel would not allow a Palestinian state in the West Bank of the Jordan River or the Gaza Strip or return East Jerusalem to the Arabs.

Khalil said, "As for the Palestinian question, the Camp David accord clearly stipulates the necessity of solving the question from all its aspects, taking into consideration the legal rights of the Palestinians. It is along this principle that they will decide their future."

In Amman, Jordan, King Hussein prepared to visit Saudi Arabia and discuss possible joint Arab action to the pending treaty.

Begin planned to leave Friday, March 23, 1979 for Washington to sign the treaty, and the Egyptian newspaper Al Ahram, said President Sadat would leave Saturday. The signing at the White House is expected Monday.

Defense Minister Ezer Weizman of Israel, brought word from Defense Secretary Harold Brown that the Carter Administration would ask congress for about 3 billion dollars to help Israel withdraw from the Sinai their air bases. New air bases will be constructed in the Negev Desert. The United States also agreed to begin delivery next year of 75 F-16 fighter planes, completing the order in 1983.

3-21-79
Israel Parliament O.K.'s treaty. Arabs scheme.

A solid majority in Israel's Parliament lined up today in support of the peace treaty with Egypt. The Saudi Arabian press meanwhile called for all-out war against Israel.

In Jidda, Saudi Arabia, a front page editorial in *Al Jezira* called today on all Arab states to prepare for a long and continuous war to regain Jerusalem and other occupied Arab land. The Palestinian resistance should fight on all fronts, "until they turn the occupied lands into a blazing inferno for the enemy."

Debate in the Knesset focused on the plan for Palestinian autonomy in the West Bank of Jordan and the Gaza Strip.

Opponents of the treaty attacked the autonomy plan as a danger to Israel's security. They said that if talks on details of the plam fail, the Middle East could drift into a new war despite the treaty.

The Labor Party said, "When the bridge collapses, we are all going to be under the rubble."

Supporters argued that peace with Egypt, despite the risks, would open a new chapter in Mid-East history.

3-22-79
Israeli Knesset's landside endorsement
Jerusalem

The Parliament of Israel endorsed the peace treaty with Egypt early today, clearing the way for Prime Minister Menachem Begin and Egyptian President Anwar Sadat to sign the historic agreement on Monday, the 26th of March in Washington, D.C.

Capping a 28-hour debate, the 120-member Knesset voted 95-18 in favor of the treaty that will end the 30-year state of war with Egypt, and pave the way for limited Palestinian autonomy on the West Bank of the Jordan River and in the Gaza Strip.

Most of those voting against the treaty were Likud Nationalists from Begin's own party, who opposed return of the Sinai and the creation of a Palestinian council. The tiny pro-Soviet Communist Party opposed the pact, claiming it did not go far enough toward Palestinian independence.

Begin told reporters that the vote was "the largest majority the Knesset has ever given on a political issue."

Egypt's 360-member Parliament will consider the accord after it is signed. The 312 members of Parliament from Sadat's National Democratic Party approved it in a caucus on March 21, 1979, ensuring passage.

A few hours after the vote, Foreign Minister Moshe Dayan from Israel, left for Washington to wrap up negotiations on a memorandum of understanding between Israel and the United States.

"The question is. . . would the United States assume the responsibility and take measures in case one of the parties would not honor the agreement?"

Defense Minister Ezer Weizman will follow Moshe Dayan to negotiate a timetable for giving up offshore oil wells the Israelis developed in the Gulf of Suez off the Sinai coast.

3-23-79
Begin urges prayers for peace
Tel Aviv, Israel

Prime Minister Menachem Begin flew to the United States today to sign the Egyptian-Israeli peace treaty and urged his people to pray for peace to spread all over the Middle East. "I pray from the bottom of my heart that this will be the first step toward a comprehensive settlement, for which we yearn. Shalom."

He repeated that he is eager to follow up the signing of the English language text of the treaty in Washington, D.C. Monday with additional ceremonies at which he and President Anwar Sadat would sign an Arabic text in Cairo, Egypt, and a Hebrew text in Jerusalem.

Sadat said this might be possible, but he still preferred to sign all three texts in Washington, because the man behind this, the Unknown Soldier, is President Carter.

Egypt said it plans to send a delegation to the West Bank and Gaza, after the signing, to try to persuade Palestinians to go along with the Palestinian autonomy plan in the accord. Talks to set up an autonomous governing body are to start late next month.

The Arab league plans to meet in Bagdad, Iraq, to decide on retaliatory action against Egypt for signing a separate peace with Israel. Mahmoud Labadi of the Popular Front for the liberation of Palestine told reporters in Beirut, Lebanon, his radical guerrilla organization will fight to defeat the "separatist" treaty, and spare no effort to undermine U.S. interests in the Arab world.

3-25-79
New Balance in Mid-East peace

Monday will mark a historic turning point in the efforts to achieve a genuine peace in the Middle East, because on that day a peace treaty between Egypt and Israel will finally be signed. In contrast to the euphoria that attended Egyptian President Anwar Sadat's visit to Jerusalem in

November, 1977, and the elation with which the Camp David Accords were greeted, the imminent signing of a peace treaty is being received with reserved satisfaction.

A stalemate that would prevail in the absence of an Egyptian-Israeli agreement would cause the radical factions against the peace accords to rise up and declare war. Israel and Egypt would drift away from their bond of friendship. The United States would be torn between its own interests in preserving a balance of power in the Mid-East to try to prevent war, and increased demands by Egypt, Jordan, and Saudi Arabia for more arms on a penalty of seeking them elsewhere.

It is conceivable that if agreement is reached regarding the West Bank and Gaza, the Syrians and Jordanians may conclude that further resistance is futile, and they may seek to negotiate a peace agreement with Israel following the model of the Egyptian-Israeli treaty. This balance may bring a comprehensive peace in the Middle East, and an end to distrust and suspicion.

3-25-79
Composition of the Mid-East treaty
Washington D.C.

This is a summary of the new Israeli-Egyptian peace treaty, how it came about, and what it means to the turbulent Middle East.

The treaty is basically a trade-off. Israel will surrender to Egypt the entire Sinai Desert, occupied since the June 1967 War, in return for peaceful relations — its first with any Arab country since Israel's birth in 1948.

It has been necessary to develop a complex formula involving a wide range of military, political and economic commitments to try to assure a trade-off will work.

The major elements of this formula are:

War

The treaty formally declares that "the state of war between the parties will be terminated and peace will be established between them." Egypt and Israel declare jointly that they "recognize and will respect each other's right to live in peace within their secure and recognized boundaries."

They also promise to refrain from the threat or use of force against one another, to settle disputes "by peaceful means" and to take steps to make sure that their territories will not be used for mounting attacks of any kind on each other.

Relations

For the Israelis, ending a state of war was only a first objective. The more basic long-term objective was to build a real peace with Egypt, including the building of trade and cultural relations, establish freedom of movement, and put end to hostile propaganda and the building of normal postal, telephone, and highway communications.

Negotiations on a trade agreement are to start within six months after the first major troop withdrawals are completed, and timetables are also spelled out for other negotiations.

The two countries are to exchange ambassadors, and thus formalize their new relationship within one month after the first Israeli withdrawals, or about 10 months after the treaty is signed.

All economic boycotts are to be terminated.

Military

Israel is to withdraw all of its military forces from the Sinai Desert within three years, in stages.

In the first stage, between three and nine months after the treaty signing, forces will be withdrawn to a line extending from a point just east of the Arab city of El Arish, on the Mediterranean, to Ras Muhamad, at the southernmost tip of the Sinai.

In recent negotiations, Israel has agreed to abandon El Arish, the largest city on the Sinai, with a population of about 43,000, within three months.

The international boundary between Egypt and Israel will be the pre-1948 boundary of the British mandate of

Palestine. For the most part, this is the present Israeli border running from the lower edge of the Gaza Strip to Elat, on the Gulf of Aquaba, along the Negev Desert. The Gaza Strip, however, will have a special status on the Israeli side of the boundary. The eventual fate of the Gaza Strip, which has a population of about 350,000 Arabs, will be determined by future negotiations.

Egypt will have full sovereignty over the Sinai, which will be divided into three military zones.

Zone 1, west of the international border and the Gulf of Aquaba, varies in width from 12 to 25 miles. It will contain United Nations forces and Egyptian civil police armed only with light weapons, and performing police functions. The number of U.N. forces has not been determined.

The second zone will comprise the entire central area of the Sinai. Egypt will be permitted to deploy up to four batallions of border police in this area, with a total strength of up to 4000 men.

The third zone, east of the Suez Canal and the Gulf of Suez, is about 30 miles deep. Egypt will be allowed a full division of troops and equipment — 22,000 soldiers and 230 tanks — in this area.

3-25-79
Composition of the Mid-East Treaty

Military

Maps showing the exact lines of these zones have not been made public. A joint Israeli-Egyptian commission is to be set up to work out precise details of Israeli withdrawals and Egyptian military movements.

On the Israeli side of the new border, a zone will be established about a mile and one-half to two miles deep in which no more than four infantry battalions and UN observers — again about 4,000 men — will be permitted.

Ten Israeli air bases on the Sinai are to be abandoned. Two of those bases are among the world's most modern tactical air bases. Egypt has agreed that the abandoned bases will be used for civilian purposes only.

Linkage

A major difficulty in treaty negotiations for many months was the question of how an Israeli-Egyptian treaty would be linked to the larger question of establishing a comprehensive peace in the Middle East.

Egyptian President Anwar Sadat insisted in the negotiations that linkage must be firm so that a start could be made on a political process to solve the Palestinian problem on the West Bank of the Jordan River and in the Gaza Strip.

The linkage issue has been tempered, the final wording of the agreement substantiates this point. It states that the two countries "set for themselves the goal of completing the negotiations within one year so that elections will be held as expeditiously as possible after agreement has been reached between the two parties."

Sinai Oil

In the final agreements, Israel dropped its demands for preferential rights to buy guaranteed quantities of Egyptian oil, provided that Egypt would sell the oil on non-discriminatory commercial terms.

The United States has agreed to extend for 15 years a five-year commitment made in 1975 to guarantee Israel's supply of oil, if it is unable to meet its needs on the world market.

Settlements

Israel agreed to abandon all of its more than 30 settlements on the Sinai, which have several thousand residents. The future of Israeli settlements on the West Bank and in Gaza, however, is not made clear in the treaty. Israeli officials have indicated that they intend to continue building settlements in these areas.

History

There is little question that the peace treaty is an outgrowth of Sadat's historic trip to Jerusalem in November, 1977.

Sadat apparently believed that his gesture in recognizing the right of Israel to exist would bring about peace. That assessment proved wrong, and negotiations repeatedly threatened to fall apart in the 16 months that followed.

In the final version of the treaty with Israel, Sadat lost most of his points. He did not obtain total Israeli withdrawal from territories occupied in the 1967 war. Israeli military forces will remain in designated areas in the West Bank and Gaza. Sadat also received no assurance that a Palestinian state would eventually be formed. Instead, a limited form of Arab self-rule has been promised by the Israelis.

The Future

Controversial questions will have to be answered in the future. The people involved will face some difficult problems as: who should participate in Arab elections, the status of Arabs in East Jerusalem, the powers of a self-governing authority, and the future of Israeli settlements on the West Bank and in Gaza.

3-26-79
Landmark treaty signed by Begin and Sadat
Washington, D.C.

On March 26, 1979, Egypt and Israel, neighbors but enemies for a generation, signed a treaty to begin a new, fragile era of peace between the Arab and the Jew.

In a solemn ceremony on the lawn of the White House, Egyptian President Anwar Sadat and Israeli Prime Minister Menachem Begin signed their names in Arabic, Hebrew, and English, to a treaty promising mutual recognition, respect, and peace.

"Peace has come," declared a beaming President Carter, whose personal intervention brought the talks back to life after they had been stalemated on details.

Carter quoted the Bible and the Koran, and he offered a personal prayer the Arabs and Jews may one day be brothers.

Sadat replied by saying, "Let there be no more bloodshed between Arabs and Israelis. Let us work together until the day comes when we can beat our swords into plowshares, and our spears into pruning hooks."

Begin agreed, "No more war. No more bloodshed; Shalom, Salaam forever."

Sadat and Begin praised President Carter. Sadat called him a true friend and a man of compassion. Begin stated that Carter's work would be remembered for generations.

After each representative had signed the treaty, they grasped each other in a three-way handshake.

In the treaty, Israel agrees to dismantle Jewish settlements and return to Egypt the vast Sinai Desert seized in the Six-Day War of 1967. Egypt agrees, for the first time, to recognize formally her Jewish neighbor as a member of the community of nations.

Agreement on the final details — the question of Israeli access to oil from wells to be surrendered to Egypt — came in a final face to face session between Sadat and Begin. Begin also agreed that within seven months Israel would return to Egypt the Sinai oilfields.

Timing of the surrender of the oilfield had been an issue through the negotiations. Egypt promised to sell oil to Israel at the world price.

In return, Egypt has recognized Israel, agreeing to an exchange of ambassadors 10 months after ratification.

Chapter 6
HISTORY OF THE PATH TO PEACE

Washington — The peace treaty between Israel and Egypt comes after more than three decades of hostility between the two countries.

1947 — November 29, U.N. General Assembly votes to abolish 1920 British mandate and partition Palestine into Jewish and Arab states. Civil strife worsens as Arabs refuse to accept the plan.

1948 — May 14, Israel, comprising about 5,500 square miles of Palestine, declares itself a state as the British pull out.
May 15, Armies of seven Arab nations attack, and seven months of bitter fighting begins.

1949 — Israel and Egypt declare a cease-fire. Israeli forces hold territory that increases the fledgling country's size by almost one-third.

1953 — June 18, Egypt becomes a republic under military junta headed by Gamal Abdel Nassar. Officers include Anwar Sadat.

1956 — Nassar nationalizes the Suez Canal
October 29, Israel launches an attack on the Sinai Peninsula and pushes toward the Suez Canal.
November 5, British and French invade Egypt, striking at Port Said, in an attempt to reverse the canal nationalization.
November 6, Under intense U.S. pressure, Israeli, British and French troops stop their advance.

1967 — May 19, U.N. forces pull back from the Sinai at the urging of Egypt, which then blockades Gulf of Aquaba and moves troops to the border with Israel.
June 5, Israel launches an attack on various fronts to start Six-Day War that ends with its forces holding Sinai Peninsula, the Syrian Golan Heights, the Gaza Strip and the West Bank of the Jordan River, including East Jerusalem.
November 22, U.N. Security Council adopts Resolution 242 calling for Israeli withdrawal from occupied territory and acceptance by both sides of existence of all countries in the area.

1970 — Nassar dies. Sadat takes over as President.

1973 — October 6, Egyptian and Syrian forces attack Israel as it marks Yom Kippur, the most important Jewish religious holiday.
November 11, Egypt and Israel sign a cease-fire.

1974 — Israel and Egypt sign an agreement separating forces along the Suez Canal.

1975 — June 5, Suez Canal reopens eight years after it was closed during the 1967 war.
October 10, Egypt and Israel sign the Sinai Accord under which Israel agrees to withdraw from 1900 square miles of territory within five months.

1977 — Menachem Begin, the former guerrilla leader of the Irgun, and his Likud coalition score upset victory in

Israeli general election over Labor Party.
November 9, Sadat tells the Egyptian parliament he is willing to visit Israel.
November 15, Begin formally invites Sadat to Jerusalem.
November 19, Sadat arrived in Jerusalem to become the first Arab leader to visit since Israel came into being. He tells Israel's parliament he accepts Israel's right to exist.
December 5, Egypt cuts diplomatic ties with peace critics Syria, Libya, Iraq, Algeria, and South Yemen.
December 16, Begin meets Carter in Washington to present Israeli plan for autonomy of the West Bank and Gaza Strip.
December 25, 26, Begin and Sadat meet in Ismalia, but fail to reach any agreements.
December 31, Egypt issues terms for settlement, including Israeli acceptance of principle of withdrawal.

1978 — January 4, Carter meets Sadat at Aswan, Egypt.
February 3, Sadat meets Carter in Washington, D.C.
March 22, Carter and Begin end two days of talks in Washington in bitter disagreement over Middle East peace moves.
September 5 to 13, Carter, Sadat, and Begin hold summit at Camp David and conclude with a "Framework for Peace."
October 12, Peace treaty negotiations open in Washington.
November 11, Secretary of State Cyrus Vance presents a draft treaty accompanied by a side letter dealing with the link between the treaty and the wider issue of Palestinian autonomy.
November 21, Israel accepts the draft but rejects the side letter.
December 12, Egypt accepts draft, if it is accompanied by side letters interpreting its view of some clauses.
December 15, Israel rejects the Egyptian proposals.
December 17, Three-month Camp David deadline for treaty passes without accord.
December 31, Israeli cabinet agrees to more talks.

1979 — February 21, Vance meets Egyptian Premier Mustafa Khalil and Israeli Foreign Minister Moshe Dayan

at Camp David.
February 25, Carter invites Khalil and Begin to Camp David.
March 1, Begin and Carter open talks in Washington.
March 5, Israeli cabinet responds positively to Begin's recommendation on new U.S. proposals, and Carter announces he will go to Israel and Egypt.
March 8, Carter talks in Cairo with Sadat, who asks for changes in U.S. compromise proposals.
March 10, Carter flies to Israel for three days of talks and reports substantial progress in last-minute meeting with Begin.
March 13, Carter meets Sadat at Cairo airport and then, after telephone conversation with Begin, announces Egypt's acceptance of compromise proposals. Begin hails achievement.
March 15, Israeli cabinet approves proposals.
March 22, Knesset approves peace treaty.
March 24, Sadat arrives in Washington for treaty signing, as Vance meets Begin in New York.
March 25, Begin arrives in Washington and sees Sadat to tie up last treaty issues.
March 26, Treaty signing ceremony takes place at White House.

Chapter 7
THE EGYPTIAN-ISRAELI PEACE TREATY

PREAMBLE OF THE PEACE PACT
BETWEEN ISRAEL AND EGYPT

Convinced of the urgent necessity of the establishment of a just, comprehensive, and lasting peace in the Middle East in accordance with Security Council Resolutions 242 and 338:

Reaffirming their adherence to the "Framework for Peace in the Middle East" agreed at Camp David, dated September 17, 1978.

Noting that the aforementioned Framework as appropriate is intended to constitute a basis for peace not only between Egypt and Israel, but also between Israel and each other Arab neighbor which is prepared to negotiate peace with it on this basis:

Desiring to bring an end the state of war between them to establish a peace in which every state in the area can live in security;

Convinced that the conclusion of a treaty of peace between Egypt and Israel is an important step in the search for comprehensive peace in the area and for the attainment of the settlement of Arab-Israeli conflict in all its aspects. Inviting the other Arab parties to this dispute to join the peace process with Israel guided by and based on the principles of the aforementioned framework;

Agree and desiring to develop friendly relations and cooperation between themselves in accordance with the United Nations Charter and the principles of international law governing international relations in times of peace;

Agree to the following provisions in the free exercise of their sovereignty, in order to implement the "Framework of the Conclusion of a Peace Treaty between Egypt and Israel."

HIGHLIGHTS OF TREATY SIGNED IN WASHINGTON
Highlights of the Egyptian-Israeli peace treaty.

War and Peace — The treaty ends the formal state of war that has existed between Egypt and Israel since the Jewish state was created in 1948.

The Sinai Peninsula — Two months after the treaty takes effect, Israeli troops will withdraw from El Arish, the Sinai administrative capital. Within seven months, Israel will give up Sinai oil fields on the Gulf of Suez.

Nine months after it takes effect, Israel will withdraw from about two-thirds of the Sinai to a point east of a running line from El Arish to Ras Muhammed at the Southernmost tip of the Sinai. Israel agrees to pull out of the Sinai completely within three years.

Diplomatic Relations—Egypt agrees to exchange ambassadors and complete full diplomatic relations after Israel's completion of the nine-month Sinai withdrawal. The treaty also provides for an end to Egypt's economic embargo of Israel, the right of Israeli-flag shipping to pass through the Suez Canal, and establishment of regular trade and cultural relations. The Gulf of Aquaba, Israel's outlet to Africa, is viewed as an international waterway. Israel is also granted the right to buy oil from the Sinai oil fields.

Palestinians — Both sides agree to open negotiations on the future shape of Palestinian autonomy one month after the treaty is signed. A nonbinding target date of one year is set for holding elections for local representative councils. Should Palestinian or Jordanian opposition make agreement on autonomy impossible on the West Bank, it is agreed that the plan will be put into effect in the Gaza Strip, which had been administered by Egypt before its capture by Israel in the 1967 war.

Outside Commitments — The treaty provides that it be binding in case of conflict with any other international obligation by either party. But an interpretive side document states that the treaty will neither prevail over any outside agreements nor be prevailed over by them. Thus, each side is allowed to interpret this provision as it sees fit. Egypt has insisted that the treaty will not alter its mutual defense commitments to other Arab states and Israel has declared that the treaty takes precedence over Cairo's other pacts.

U.S. Commitments

In two memoranda negotiated with Israel separate from the treaty, the United States agrees to supply oil to Israel for 15 years should Israel declare that it is suffering a shortage as a result of relinquishing the Sinai fields. Washington also affirms to political and diplomatic support of Israel should the treaty be violated by Cairo.

Chapter 8
CONCLUSION

March 26, 1979

Today Israel and Egypt are at peace. After thirty years of war with the Arab nation of Egypt, the Israelis can breathe a sigh of relief and thank the United States and President Carter and the negotiation teams. The leaders of Egypt, Sadat and his parliament, and Begin and the Knesset can now prepare for a comprehensive peace in the Middle East. To make the peace treaty workable, it must be monitored and implemented in all areas of the Middle East.

There are many enemies to the peace accord. Radical Arab League antagonists met in Baghdad, Iraq to form a coalition, a possible embargo against the United States and Egypt.

Farouk Kaddoumi, head of the PLO's political department stated that the Palestinians have "nothing to lose. From today we will not hesitate to take any action against America and U.S. interests."

Delegations from Syria, Libya, and the Palestine Liberation Organization have called for an extensive boycott against Egypt, as well as its suspension from the Arab League, and for moving the league's headquarters out of Cairo.

Extreme measures have been resisted by "soft liners," led by Saudi Arabia. The Saudi Foreign Minister Saud Al Faisal has taken the view that the diplomatic relationship between the Arab countries is a sovereign matter, not something to be acted upon at an international conference.

Meanwhile, Secretary of State Cyrus Vance gave assurance to Egypt that the United States has "no intention whatsoever" of stationing U.S. military forces in the Sinai Desert as part of a commitment to consider aiding Israel if Egypt violates the recently signed peace treaty. The memorandum of understanding states that "the United States will consider a variety of options to deal with any treaty violation." It relates only to threats of the peace with both nations.

I forecast that peace and prosperity will come to the Middle East. The Palestinian refugee situation will improve, and the people in the settlements will be permitted to expand into the greater Sinai. They will be allowed to develop agriculture, industries, businesses, or homes of their own.

I predict that the people may form governments of their own, and plan their own way of life in freedom.

Only time will heal the wounds of suspicion and distrust. Faith and hope for a better world, and everlasting peace can be accomplished by determination and perseverance and loyalty to high aims and ambitions.

THE END

BIBLIOGRAPHY OF SOURCE MATERIAL

A. Books
Bermant, Chaim. *Israel.* Walker and Company, 1967.

B. Articles
"Menachem Begin." *Current Biography.* H.W. Wilson Company, 1977.

"James Carter." *Current Biography.* H.W. Wilson Company, 1971.

"Anwar El Sadat." *Current Biography.* H.W. Wilson Company, 1971.

"Cyrus R. Vance." *Current Biography.* H.W. Wilson Company, 1977.

U.S. Department of State Bulletin. *Camp David Agreements,* by Harold H. Saunders. Washington, D.C.: Government Printing Office, November, 1978.

U.S. Department of State Bulletin. *Middle East,* by Alfred R. Atherton Jr. Washington, D.C.: Government Printing Office, May, 1978.

U.S. Department of State Bulletin. *Egypt and Israel Sign Treaty of Peace.* Washington, D.C.: Government Printing Office, May, 1979.

U.S. Department of State Bulletin. *Framework for Middle East Peace*. Washington, D.C.: Government Printing Office, October, 1978.

Los Angeles Times. "The Peace Treaty," March 26, 1979.

C. Newspapers
Long Beach Press Telegram. 1977-1979.
Los Angeles Times. 1977-1979.
The Register, Santa Ana, California. 1977-1979.

ABOUT THE AUTHOR

CLETE A. HINTON was born in a railroad town outside of Chicago, Illinois. His family moved to Topeka, Kansas, where he attended elementary and junior high school. He moved to California in the early 1940s. He was active in sports and excelled in pole vaulting and track. He went to several schools in Southern California including R.O.T.C. at Poly High School in Long Beach. He graduated from Compton, California, in 1943.

Mr. Hinton served in the United States Navy during World War II from 1943 to 1946. He joined the Los Angeles County Fire Department in August of 1949, and his illustrious career continued for twenty-eight years. He retired from the fire department as an engineer in March of 1978. After his retirement, Mr. Hinton became a newspaper reporter working primarily in the high desert, Apple Valley, Victorville, and Hesperia. He is currently working on a manuscript entitled *Firefighting in the Trenches*.

www.ingramcontent.com/pod-product-compliance
Lightning Source LLC
Chambersburg PA
CBHW070521100426
42743CB00010B/1894